TAXIDERMY

TAXIDERMY

Leon L. Pray

NEW YORK

THE
MACMILLAN
COMPANY

THE MACMILLAN COMPANY, NEW YORK
PRINTED IN THE UNITED STATES OF AMERICA

TABLE OF CONTENTS

INTRODUCTION

Taxidermy in these modern times, with borax mothproofing as its latest and greatest step forward, can be a fascinating hobby, well able to fill in many spare hours with undreamed-of satisfaction. After a lifetime as a professional taxidermist in all branches, this writer can heartily recommend the practice of arsenic-free taxidermy to people of a naturalistic bent. Some may desire to become professionals, but more may wish to retain their keen zest by plying this art as a pastime only, in hours of relaxation. It is to such readers that this book is particularly offered.

Professional taxidermy is apt to develop into a grind, with its aesthetic values growing dulled in the rush of required production. On the other hand, the taxidermy hobbyist should be able to retain his primary enthusiasm because of the fact that he works for himself and solely for the thrill of it, with little worry about material necessities. There is real satisfaction to be found in collecting, mounting, and arranging a personal collection of animal specimens.

The assembling of a taxidermist's workshop is a pleasure to contemplate. The unused half of a double garage, a corner in a well-lighted basement, a snug attic room, or best of all, of course, a specially constructed shop, may be used to accommodate the amateur. I fondly recall my first workroom. It was partitioned off in the southeast corner of the hayloft of our barn. A small wood-burning stove was installed, and a long workbench occupied half of one wall. Shelves were conveniently built in above the bench. An electric globe furnished light when the sun did not; a horizontal window lighted the workbench and afforded a view besides.

This boyhood shop became a mecca to my pals. The bench seat and extra chair were seldom vacant when taxidermy work was going on. Here innumerable birds and small mammals were stuffed. Here my first deer heads were mounted by use of the cleaned skull and excelsior method of those times. If I could then have known borax mothproofing, as I have developed and perfected it during the past thirty years, my early experience would have been completely happy. As it was, arsenical methods came near to being my finish.

Other great improvements are now to be found. Well-built paper deer-head forms are one of today's outstanding aids to better taxidermy. These are a standard product. Along with the head forms, ear liners, skin paste, glass eyes, wall shields, and all the things needed for a good job of mounting game heads may be purchased ready for use. Look through the catalog of a reputable dealer in taxidermy supplies and read the lists of tools and accessories presented for sale. Glass eyes, once strictly a European product, are now made even better in America.

At the start, before buying costly additions to his tool kit, the beginner should try to produce good work with a simple home outfit. It is better to buy cautiously so as not to invest in unnecessary equipment.

Study this book, then try your hand, and know the thrill that comes from doing work which at the same time can be stimulating recreation.

LEON L. PRAY

TAXIDERMY

CHAPTER I

TOOLS AND MATERIALS

The necessary tools with which to do taxidermy can be named in a comparatively brief list. My beginners' tools and materials were:

1 claw hammer
1 tack hammer
1 cross-cut saw
1 rip saw
1 pair common shears
1 pair small scissors
1 pocket knife
1 paring knife
1 pair tweezers
1 pair side-cutting pliers

Ball twine
Needles and thread
Nails, tacks, and staple-tacks
Scrap lumber
Cotton batting
Tow
Excelsior
Assorted galvanized wire
Plaster-of-Paris
Glue
Oil paints and brushes
Glass eyes

Using this outfit, I turned out a lot of creditable work, though many a modern lad might feel that such a layout would cramp his style.

Tabulated for consideration are:

1 large Bernard side-cutting pliers
1 small Bernard side-cutting pliers
1 small pointed-nosed pliers
1 long-handled rod-cutter
1 large tinners' shears
1 small tinners' shears
1 small scissors

1 tap and die, thread cutting set, 3/16 to ½-inch dies
1 surgeons' bone-snips
1 surgeons' scalpel
1 surgeons' cartilage knife
1 kitchen paring knife
1 butchers' skinning knife
1 toothed grapefruit knife. (To be used in scraping small skins.)
1 fine oilstone and can of oil
Round needles, assorted sizes up to darning needle
Three-cornered needles, assorted sizes
Several sizes of cotton and linen thread
Ball twine
Twine holder. (A perforated coffee can will do.)
1 dozen cotton "cops." (This is the standard soft thread for wrapping birds.)
1 small trowel
1 small plaster tool or spatula
2 or 3 wooden modeling tools
1 coarse steel fur comb
1 fine steel fur comb
1 small ball-peen hammer
1 claw hammer
1 cross-cut saw
1 rip saw
1 hack saw
1 coping saw
1 drill set
1 upholsterers' regulator or spindle
1 pair fine-tipped tweezers
Several sizes mill files
1 medium fine wood rasp
1 skin scraper for use on large skins
1 large stuffing rod
1 small stuffing rod. (Make stuffing rods from heavy wire and light rod by hammering one end flat, then filing coarse teeth on the front edge. Bend a loop handle on the other end.)
Several sizes of bristle and sable artists' brushes, both flat and round shapes
1 pint purified linseed oil
1 pint purified turpentine
1 tube each, tube oil color, white, black, cadmium red, cadmium yel-

low, raw and burnt sienna, raw and burnt umber, yellow ochre, terra rosa, permanent blue, viridian green. (Add to the list as required.)

A few small dishes to mix paints in

1 quart butyl acetate for cleaning paint brushes and dishes

A few yards of absorbent cheesecloth for dust and paint rags and for damp-wrapping mounting work

Several yards of cheap oilcloth for damp-wrapping

Powdered borax. (Buy from the producer, in 100-lb. lots, and save a lot of money.)

100 lbs. plaster-of-Paris. (Buy from the manufacturer, if possible, and save.)

Tow. (Tow costs approximately $80 a bale and can be purchased in small lots from taxidermy supply houses.)

Excelsior. (Buy by the bale, jewelers' grade.)

Excelsior. (Buy by the bale, coarse grade.)

Cotton batting. (For general fine wrapping work use the best long-fiber grade. For stuffing, buy the large batts of coarse gray shoddy type. This stuffs easier and lies better where placed.)

Commercial glass eyes. (Buy as needed. Large stocks of eyes will lie around indefinitely and are generally no investment. They are expensive and tie up funds.)

Hardware cloth (galvanized wire netting) of ¼ and ½-inch mesh. (If you are going to build home-made wire-cloth head forms or mannikins. Buy in amounts only as needed.)

Galvanized iron wire. (Buy as needed, without tying up cash in quantity, if hardware stocks are handy.)

Casein water paint, in powder or paste form

Casein glue

White flour. (For making paste.)

White cornmeal. (To be used when skinning for table meat.)

Yellow petroleum wax. (Hard grade, for waxing lips, etc. Half as costly as beeswax, and better.)

Clean, dry sifted sand

1 nest of crockery mixing bowls

1 double cereal cooker. (1-quart size, for melting wax.)

Large and small spoons

Salt. (For double-salting fresh skins to keep prior to leathering. Table salt for small skins, dairy salt for large skins.)

3

CHAPTER II

PREPARING AND MOUNTING A DEER HEAD

In this chapter a game head is given first place because of the great popularity and appeal of trophies of this kind. Mounted game heads stand up well under the rigors of time and exposure to dust. They are easily cleaned, either by direct washing or by rubbing down with cornmeal or dry borax. The essentials of having a perfect mounted head for a wall piece or a pedestal mount are first to be observed at the hunting camp. Many a fine deer scalp has been ruined and lost on account of not being skinned out and properly salted while absolutely fresh.

Preparations for mounting a game head should begin before the head is skinned, in the hunting field if possible. Make neck circumference measurements. Sketch and photograph the specimen. If possible, lay the head and neck on a large piece of brown paper and draw a contact outline of it with a black crayon. Pose the head and neck on its side in several positions and record each attitude with a contact outline. Lay the specimen on an old blanket to keep it clean while skinning; a litter of forest rubbish results in a miserable job.

Study the illustrations showing the making of correct incisions for skinning. Insert the knife point under the skin with the edge of the knife upward, and push it along, making a clean incision that will loosen no hair. At the apex of the Y cut shown in the drawing, branch off to the base of one antler. Return to the apex of the Y cut and proceed to the base of the other antler. Return to the shoulder incision. Lift one point of skin on top of the shoulders and proceed to peel off the neck skin. Be care-

Fig. 1

BROWN PAPER SKETCHES OF A DEER HEAD

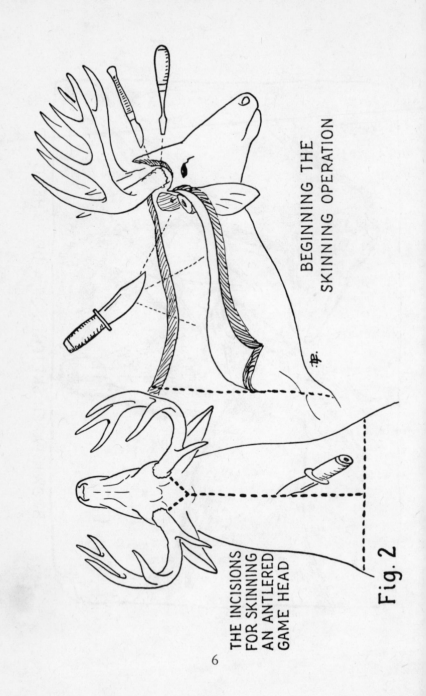

BEGINNING THE
SKINNING OPERATION

THE INCISIONS
FOR SKINNING
AN ANTLERED
GAME HEAD

Fig. 2

6

ful to hold the edge of the knife more toward the flesh than the skin, to avoid cutting holes in the skin. Naturally, a perfect scalp is the requirement of the taxidermist.

When the head is reached, cut the ear butts away close to the skull. Skin around the antlers with a smaller knife. Do not haggle the skin at its margin under the antler burrs. Work slowly and use patience. A not-too-sharp blade is useful here, prying the skin free rather than slicing. A screw driver is also good.

Approach the eye sockets cautiously, peeling the skin free, with the knife close to the bone. When the corners of the mouth are encountered, sever the lip lining close to the jaw bones. Sever the snout close to the skull bones, leaving all of the cartilaginous tip of the nose attached to the skin. Peel the end of the nose out carefully to retain the nostril linings. Split the lips to their edges. Go slowly.

When the scalp or cape (as the head and neck skin is called) is freed from the deer, skin out the butts and backs of the ears. Proceed with extra caution, using a dull spatulate tool in the backs of the ears. A little smooth hardwood paddle is ideal for this job. Clean the meat from the butts of the ear cartilages. Leave the cartilages attached in the skin by their front surfaces. Split the eyelid linings to their edges. Use great care here.

Spread the scalp, flesh side up, flat on a floor or blanket. Shave off all lumps of meat and fat with a broad-bladed knife. Pour a pile of salt on the middle of the scalp. Begin pushing and rubbing the salt outward to the edges of the skin until every detail has been rubbed full of salt.

Roll up the scalp, first folding the sides inward, flesh to flesh. Put it on a sloping board in a cool place to drain overnight. Next day spread the scalp and scrape all of the first salting completely out of every detail. Shake the scalp and spread it flat again, flesh side up. Pour a pile of fresh salt on the middle, and push and rub the salt into every detail again. Fold the sides in, roll up and store until it is sent to a taxidermists' tanner for finishing. Consider no other kind of tanner for this work.

7

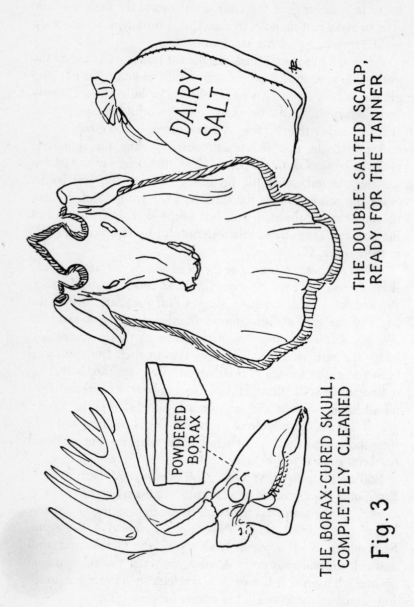

THE BORAX-CURED SKULL, COMPLETELY CLEANED

POWDERED BORAX

THE DOUBLE-SALTED SCALP, READY FOR THE TANNER

DAIRY SALT

Fig. 3

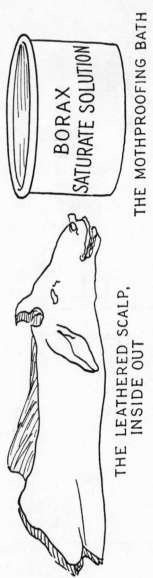

THE LEATHERED SCALP,
INSIDE OUT

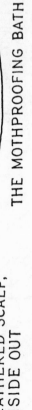

BORAX
SATURATE SOLUTION

THE MOTHPROOFING BATH

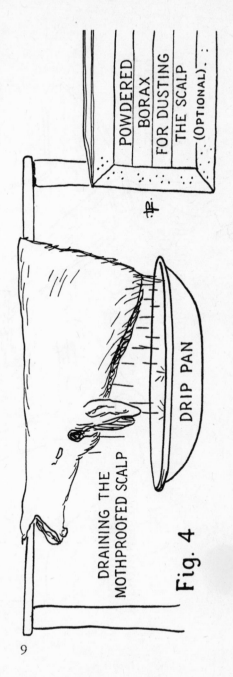

POWDERED
BORAX
FOR DUSTING
THE SCALP
(OPTIONAL)

DRIP PAN

DRAINING THE
MOTHPROOFED SCALP

Fig. 4

9

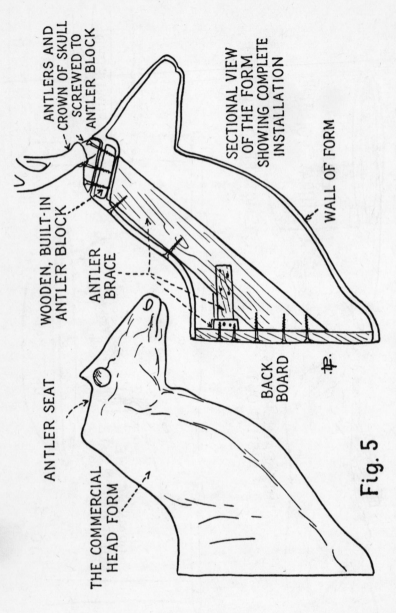

ANTLERS AND CROWN OF SKULL SCREWED TO ANTLER BLOCK

WOODEN, BUILT-IN ANTLER BLOCK

ANTLER BRACE

SECTIONAL VIEW OF THE FORM SHOWING COMPLETE INSTALLATION

WALL OF FORM

ANTLER SEAT

THE COMMERCIAL HEAD FORM

BACK BOARD

Fig. 5

10

A description of the process of tanning, or leathering, a deer scalp is best omitted here, for it would require a volume by itself. No short description could comprehensively cover the subject, and an amateur taxidermist would scarcely care to attempt so detailed and exacting a job. The price for leathering is reasonable enough to fit the average customer's purse. There is such a great difference in quality between a raw skin mount and a leathered job that there should be no hesitation over which to choose. A raw skin mount will burst open in a short time and be ready for the scrap heap, also, shrinkage is unsightly.

When ordering head forms from a manufacturer, send the circumference measurement of the deer necks, also the lineal measurement of faces from front of eye socket to end of nose. These figures give a clue to sizes of forms required. Be sure that the head forms have built-in antler blocks. Forms may be purchased with or without installed back-boards. It is best to install a back-board in the shoulders with a wooden brace screwed to the back-board, leading up through the neck against the under side of the antler block, if the antlers are heavy. The brace should also be against the inside back of the neck. Such a brace is important if the head form is not of extra-heavy construction.

If the antlers are of light weight, with the back-board properly glued and nailed in place, the internal wooden brace may be left out. Take no chances of the weight of the scalp and antlers or of large sheep horns tearing the form from the back-board, when finally hung on a wall. Mountain sheep horns are as heavy as stone, and big deer antlers are often almost as bad.

Do not begrudge a fair price for first-class head forms. Bargain head forms are like bargain cigars—both are loaded with trouble. A good head-form maker and a good taxidermists' tanner are a great help.

After receiving the leathered scalp, the head form, and ear liners, the next consideration is to mothproof the scalp permanently. To make borax saturate solution, use four ounces of borax per gallon of water. Agitate the water briskly while sift-

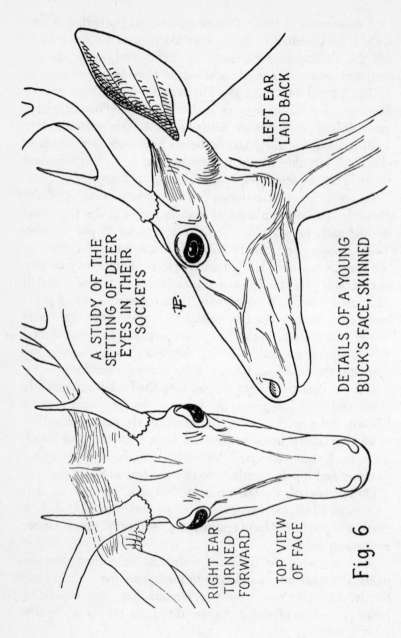

LEFT EAR
LAID BACK

A STUDY OF THE
SETTING OF DEER
EYES IN THEIR
SOCKETS

DETAILS OF A YOUNG
BUCK'S FACE, SKINNED

RIGHT EAR
TURNED FORWARD

TOP VIEW
OF FACE

Fig. 6

ing the borax in slowly, and stir until all of the powder is dissolved. Make enough to cover the scalp. Immerse the scalp, and stir and agitate it in the liquid. Let it stand awhile, then plunge and agitate it again. Give it an hour or so of soaking, then squeeze it out of the liquid and hang it over a pole to drain, hair outward. A scalp so treated is moth proofed forever, in every particle of its structure. When the scalp is well drained, it may be immediately mounted, or it may be hung up on a line by its shoulder margin, with clothespins, and dried for later mounting. Store it anywhere without fear of insect damage.

Skulls soaked in borax solution and dried will not harbor dermestids or bacon beetles. When a scalp is kept dried after mothproofing, it should be relaxed for mounting by moistening it on the inside with borax solution.

Making the head form ready

Given a well-made form on which to mount the deer scalp, it is necessary to do a few things preliminary to the actual work of mounting. Screw a length of pine 1 x 2-inch strip (or heavier if needed) on the back-board, as shown in the drawings. This is for the purpose of setting the form in a vise. After placing the form in the vise, tilted at a low angle, check the skull top, measuring the amount of bone frontlet to be sawed from the skull with the antlers, for fitting accurately on the form. When the frontlet, or skull plate, is sawed from the skull, drill three or four screw holes through the crown. Screw the antlers in place on the form, using 3-inch wood screws. Make up ½ pint or more of papier-mâché. Model this around the skull plate on top of the form. This work should be done long enough before the day of mounting the scalp so that the papier-mâché has time to dry hard. Set glass eyes in the eye sockets. Hold the eyes in place with a few pins pushed in around them while the papier-mâché is placed and drying. In setting the eyes, remember that a deer can look straight forward, as well as being able to turn its eyes in any direction.

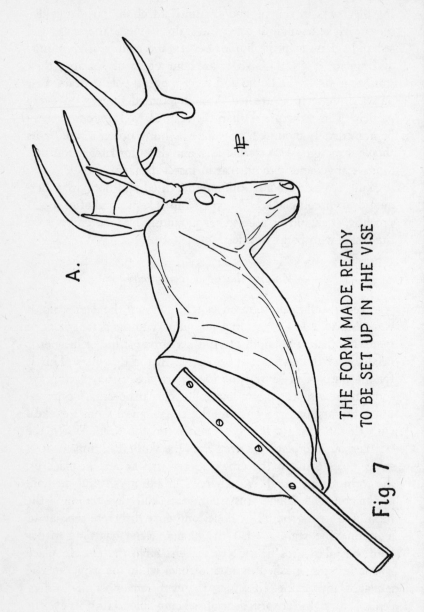

A.

Ŧ

THE FORM MADE READY
TO BE SET UP IN THE VISE

Fig. 7

14

With a small drill make a ring of holes in the bone just under the antler burrs, for the purpose of nailing the skin snugly under the burrs.

Making the scalp ready

Check the scalp for any needed repairs. Sew up any cut holes around the eyes and lips, using small stitches. Use the baseball stitch and finish the seam with a close knot. The baseball stitch is made by passing the needle and thread through the skin from the under or flesh side and out on the outside for each stitch. After making three or four stitches, pause and pull them up snugly before proceeding.

The scalp should be entirely softened by sponging inside of it with borax solution. Allow the first application to soak in, then repeat and sponge until the leathered scalp is soft and stretchable in all its parts. Stretch especially the width of the neck to make it ready for the form.

Give the scalp a preliminary fitting on the form. Pull with the fingers under the skin so as to not pull on the hair. Throughout the work of mounting, never pull on the hair at all. Casein glue extended with flour paste and bug-proofed by the addition of a little powdered borax makes a satisfactory skin paste for uniting the leathered scalp to the head form. A wide flat bristle brush is used for spreading the paste on the form and skin. Put no paste on the scalp or form before trying the scalp on. Stretch the scalp to fit easily over all dimensions of the form, including the eyelids, lips, nostril linings, ear butts. Even the ear skin should now be spread by careful stretching.

When you are satisfied with the trial fitting, brush paste into the ear skins. Slip the ear liners in place, and press the skin gently into contact with the liners. See that the edges of the ears are accurately fitted over the edges of the liners. Paper ear liners may be trimmed and beveled if they do not fit exactly. It is well to have several sizes of ear liners on hand.

15

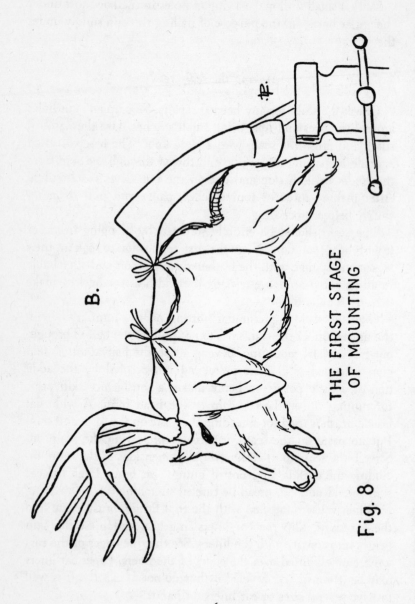

B.

F.

THE FIRST STAGE
OF MOUNTING

Fig. 8

Next brush paste all over the inside of the face skin. Slip the face skin over the face of the head form, and mold the skin into place. Work out all air bubbles from under the skin. Apply light pressure so as not to squeeze the paste around unevenly, or entirely away from some areas. Draw the neck skin into place on the form and tie it temporarily with twine, with no paste applied to the neck skin as yet.

Center the white throat patch correctly. Make up about a pint of papier-mâché, rather thick. Model the ear butts out with papier-mâché over a small wad of twine-wrapped excelsior for a core in each, if the liners were made without built-in butts. Use care not to make the ear butts too large or too small. Sharpen one end of each of two pieces of heavy wire, 16 inches long. Push these through the ear openings from outside. Set the ears on the head at the correct angle to give the expression desired. Drive the wires through the head-form wall with the points slanting downward and pricked into the opposite wall so that the ears will be supported by them resting under the upper flanges of the ears. These supports are to be left in until the head is dry. Secure the ears to them by sewing through the ears and tying them to the wires. Press the ear butt filling into natural shape. If the ears are set forward, see that the wrinkles are natural and evenly distributed on the forward sides of the butts. If the ear liners included built-in butts, a few small nails around their edges and a little papier-mâché are required to fix them in place, but it is more satisfactory to use the wire supports as well. All built-in ear butts need some paring to make them fit the head form accurately.

Next brush paste under the skin of the crown of the head. Draw the scalp snugly up around under the antler burrs. Secure the edges in place under the burrs with small nails driven through the skin into the holes previously bored in the bone under the burrs. Use nails that will fit the holes tightly.

With a sharp-edged sack needle and doubled waxed thread, pick up a point of the scalp at the center of the Y incision on the

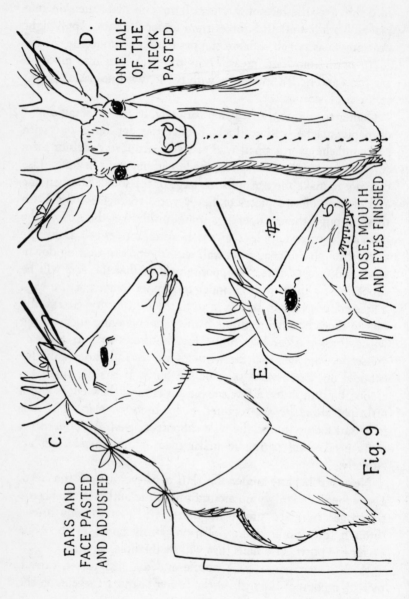

D.

ONE HALF OF THE NECK PASTED

C.

EARS AND FACE PASTED AND ADJUSTED

E.

NOSE, MOUTH AND EYES FINISHED

Fig. 9

back of the head. Sew one arm of the Y from its apex to the antler and knot it securely. Sew all incisions in mammal and bird skin work from the rear of the incision forward. This keeps the hair or plumage from falling over the seam when each stitch is drawn up.

Mold the skin on top of the deer head carefully into position. Place the median line of the front of the neck skin along the center of the neck of the form. Tack along it with a row of small sharp nails about 3 inches apart. Remove the twine ties from the neck. Let the skin hang on the row of nails. Catch up one side of the neck skin and tack it to the top of the neck temporarily. Paste the other half of the neck skin, cover that side of the form with paste, and apply the skin to it. Let down the other half. Paste and apply. Mold the skin down with the fingers, working out any air bubbles. Draw the rear edge of the skin over the back edge of the form and tack it temporarily to the back-board with a few small sharp nails, not driven all the way in.

Draw the long incision together on top of the neck. Tie it in three places with single-tied stitches, evenly spaced to hold the skin edges accurately while the incision is being sewn up. Sew the long incision from its back end toward the Y cut on top of the head. Draw all stitches up tightly as each three or four are taken. If the skin is extra tough and hard to sew, it may be perforated by using a belt punch and making opposite holes ½ inch apart along the cut edges. Lace it up like a shoe, using two waxed twine ends with two tape needles. This method may have more appeal to the average operator. Pick hair out of stitches as you proceed.

After the long neck incision is sewn up, inspect the face, ears, and neck. Use an upholsterer's regulator, or spindle, to pick and push the skin smoothly over the form.

Fill the eyelids with just enough papier-mâché to model them to natural shape. Press the pre-orbital gland pits into place. Mold the nostrils into the nose details of the form. (All first-class modern head forms include mouth and nose details.) With a good

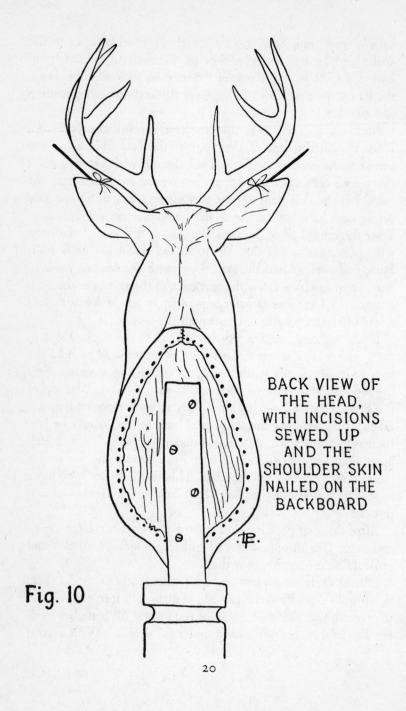

BACK VIEW OF
THE HEAD,
WITH INCISIONS
SEWED UP
AND THE
SHOULDER SKIN
NAILED ON THE
BACKBOARD

Fig. 10

head form and a properly leathered scalp, little or no pinning or nailing will be required. Push the lips into place so that the black lip markings are alike on both sides. A small bristle brush is handy for pasting the face details. The lips may be tacked in place with a row of pins until dry. Tuck the lips in neatly, then drive the pins through their edges deep in the mouth groove. A smooth hardwood modeling tool is used to mold the facial details into shape. If a groove for receiving the lips is lacking, such a groove should be cut in with a knife before the lips are pasted.

Use the thumbs and fingers mainly in adjusting the ear skins on the liners. Stuff a loose wad of excelsior into the hollow of each ear to hold the skin in place until dry.

Go over all facial details again. Too much care cannot be exercised before the head is left to begin drying. Also go over the neck once more, feeling for any overlooked air bubbles. These will make a crackling sound when pushed around in the paste. Spear each bubble with the point of a knife held parallel to the grain of the hair so as not to cut off any hair. Do not press hard enough to squeeze paste out. Paste on the hair may be washed out with a sponge and borax water.

Remove the head from the vise, and set it upon its antlers. Unscrew the support from the back-board. With a sharp knife trim excess skin from the border which overlaps the back-board. Remove the temporary nailing. Adjust the edge of the skin evenly, pasting and nailing it permanently. Place the small flat-headed nails near the edge of the skin. The skin flap should be about 1½ inches wide, with the nailing spaced ¼ inch in from the edge of the skin and an inch apart. Shear the hair off from the nailed overlapping skin flap.

When the skin is all nailed on the back-board, replace the support and again set the head in the vise. Check over all details once more. Make sure of accuracy of adjustment of the white face markings and throat patch. Unsymmetrical markings will spoil the looks of an otherwise good mount. Work on the eyes until an expression of alive interest is secured. Give special atten-

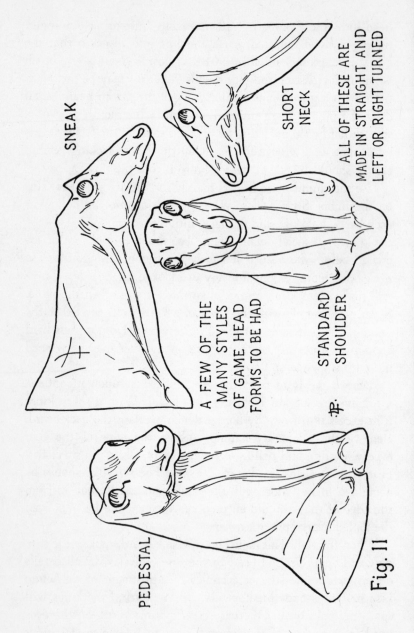

SNEAK

SHORT
NECK

ALL OF THESE ARE
MADE IN STRAIGHT AND
LEFT OR RIGHT TURNED

A FEW OF THE
MANY STYLES
OF GAME HEAD
FORMS TO BE HAD

STANDARD
SHOULDER

PEDESTAL

Fig. 11

tion to the nose and lips. Allow no lip or nostril lining to show where it should not.

When all adjusting is completed, it is a good idea to remove the support and hang the head up by its antlers so that all of the skin may dry out at once. If dried on the support or hung with the back-board against a wall, the skin on that part of the back-board which is covered will not dry out with the rest of the head. Hanging by the antlers is safe only if the head form is well made.

Hang the head free, with air circulating all around it. Inspect the details daily. A little attention with a modeling tool will keep the skin and papier-mâché drying evenly so that no distortion should result. Comb and brush the hair of the mount before hanging it up to dry. Allow the head to dry out completely before retouching colors of the bare skin and waxing certain details.

When dry, replace the head on the support in the vise. Shave a little hard yellow petroleum wax. Cover the wax shavings with benzine overnight. When the wax is soft, mix the wax and benzine together to make a wax cream as thick as vaseline. To make it smooth, squeeze it through two layers of cheesecloth. Keep in a tight container. Take a little of the wax cream and color it with a small amount of burnt umber oil color. Mix it thoroughly to diffuse the color. Apply the colored wax around the inside edges of the eyelids and deep inside the nostrils with a small brush. Keep the wax away from the facial hair. Allow the wax to partly dry out, then model it into shape. Tool a bit of it into the pre-orbital glands. Color the bare skin of the nose tip and around the eye corners with the wax cream, rubbing it in with a small brush. Clean off any that gets on the hair with a cloth dampened, but not wet, with benzine.

Color some of the wax cream flesh-tinted with just a drop of Venetian red oil color. Pull out the ear rods with a twisting motion, and remove the excelsior wads. Brush the inside of the ears clean. If the skin shows among the hair, color it with the flesh-colored wax cream. Pin the white hair inside the ears back out

THE STEPS IN BUILDING A HOMEMADE DEER HEAD
FORM OF WOOD, HARDWARE CLOTH, AND PAPIER-MACHE

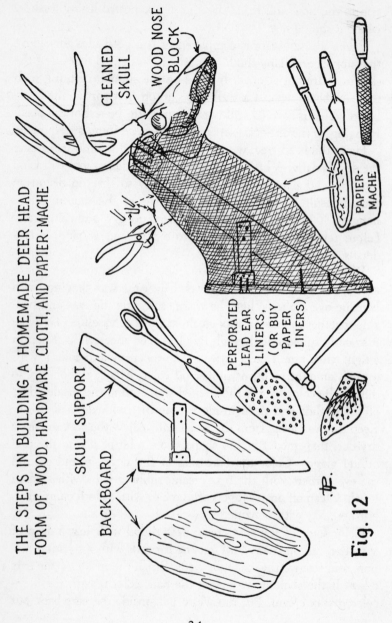

CLEANED SKULL

WOOD NOSE BLOCK

PAPIER-MACHE

SKULL SUPPORT

BACKBOARD

PERFORATED LEAD EAR LINERS, (OR BUY PAPER LINERS)

Fig. 12

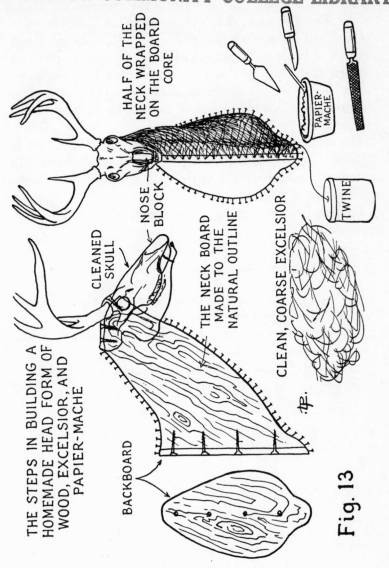

THE STEPS IN BUILDING A HOMEMADE HEAD FORM OF WOOD, EXCELSIOR, AND PAPIER-MACHE

HALF OF THE NECK WRAPPED ON THE BOARD CORE

PAPIER-MACHE

TWINE

NOSE BLOCK

CLEANED SKULL

THE NECK BOARD MADE TO THE NATURAL OUTLINE

CLEAN, COARSE EXCELSIOR

BACKBOARD

Fig. 13

25

of the way while applying the colored wax. Clean from the hair with a benzine-dampened rag. (Better use extreme care not to get the colored wax on the hair in the first place.)

Comb and brush the head all over again. Rub the hair down with a wad of clean cheesecloth. This is the only "polish" that museum specimens ever receive. Borax-cured hair retains its natural luster. Some commercial mothproofing preparations eat away the glossy, natural surface of the hair, leaving it dead and lusterless.

The deer head may now be screwed on a heraldic shield, or on an oblong panel with a frame border, or it may be fitted with a strap-iron hanger with a "keyhole" at the top to hang it directly against a wall.

Illustrated tips for making a home-made deer-head form accompany this chapter.

Suggested procedure for deer-head mounting

1) Get scalp and form ready one day. Roll mothproofed scalp in oilcloth overnight, or hang over a pole if it is very moist.

2) Next day mount neck, ears, and face. Cover face with borax-damp cloths overnight.

3) Next day finish facial details, i.e., mouth, nose, and eyelids, rechecking ears in the same job.

CHAPTER III

PREPARING AND MOUNTING A FISH

PART ONE

The black bass provides an ideal mounting subject. In general, the hard-scaled kinds of fishes are to be preferred for mounting, i.e., the sunfishes, perch, pickerel, muskellunge, gars, and many varieties of near-shore ocean fishes. Those kinds with much fat make poor taxidermy specimens. In modern museum work all fishes are cast and models are made up with celluloid fins and oil paint colors added. This kind of mounting does not appeal to the sportsman as a trophy for his den. He wants "the real thing" or nothing to be hung on his walls.

When beginning the preparatory work for mounting a fish, look the specimen over carefully. Choose the more perfect, undamaged side for show. Spread a piece of brown paper on the table, and pose the fish on the paper, better side up. Hold a pencil upright against the fish and trace around it, making a contact outline sketch of the whole specimen, including the fins, held spread as you wish them to be on the mount. With thumb and pencil measure the width of the body, from side to side, in about five or six places along it. Put these diameters in lines along the sketch where they belong.

Lay the fish on its better side on the dampened table top, or on wet oilcloth. Make an incision with shears, the full length of mid-side from the tail fin to the joint in the shoulder girdle. Use tinners' shears on a heavy skin. Cut through the shoulder hinge with a cartilage knife.

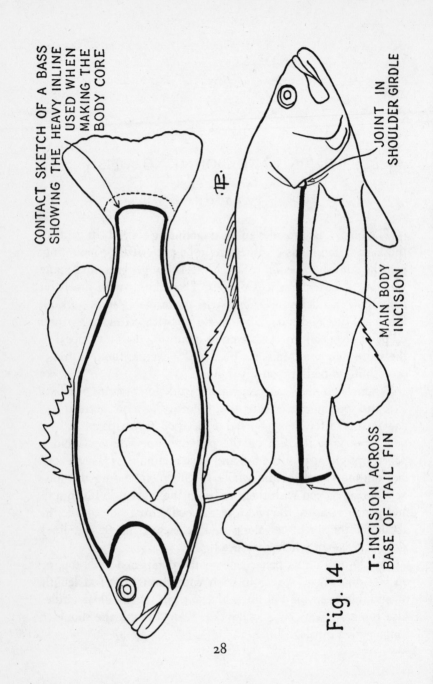

CONTACT SKETCH OF A BASS
SHOWING THE HEAVY INLINE
USED WHEN
MAKING THE
BODY CORE

JOINT IN
SHOULDER GIRDLE

MAIN BODY
INCISION

T-INCISION ACROSS
BASE OF TAIL FIN

Fig. 14

28

Leave the fish lying flat as much as possible while skinning. That is, the skin should lie on the table and the body should be maneuvered out of it. Do not bend the skin endwise. Sidewise turning of the skin from the incision does no harm, but endwise rolling of a fish skin breaks the epidermis and forces scales out of their sockets.

Make a cross-incision along the end of the tail fin where the skin joins it. Lay the corners back and cut through the base of the fin bones with bone-snips. Use care not to damage the skin of the other side of the tail. Prepare to remove the body from the skin; use a dull knife for the job. Peel the end of the tail free from the skin. Lift the tail and bend it gradually forward and up from the skin, then lay the tail down. Peel the skin of the side away from the body on each side of the long incision until the center of the back and belly are reached.

Dissect a considerable amount of the fin-bone roots out and cut them free from the body, leaving ¼ or ½ inch of the roots intact on the fins.

Again lift the end of the tail and proceed to separate the body from the prone skin. It is handy to have an assistant to hold the body of a large fish while the operator gives his entire attention to the skinning job. When the skin is freed as far as the shoulder girdle, lay the carcass back in the skin. Using heavy shears and bone-snips, cut the body free from the skin at the shoulder girdle. Leave unbroken the point of attachment of the chest at the throat. Lay the skinned body on the brown paper alongside the superficial contact sketch, and make a contact outline of it.

With a curved scraper-tip remove the eyeballs. Cut around inside the rims of the eye sockets to open the way for removing the cheek muscles. Use a round-ended table knife to release the cheek skin from the meat, and a curved scraper to remove the cheek meat. Leave the skull whole, except the brain case. Nip this out with bone-snips. Scrape forward in the face in front of the eye sockets and remove all of the fat and gristly material there. Scrape the skull bones clean, and rub dry borax in. Leave

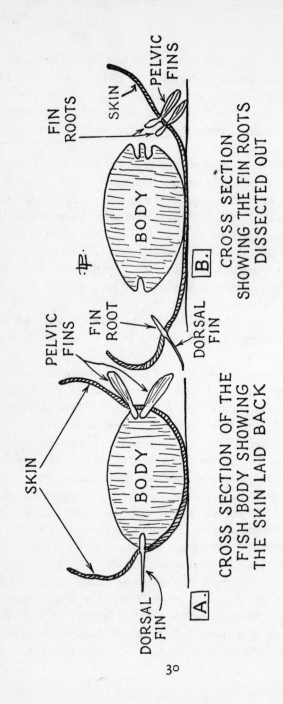

SKIN

DORSAL FIN

PELVIC FINS

FIN ROOT

BODY

A. CROSS SECTION OF THE FISH BODY SHOWING THE SKIN LAID BACK

FIN ROOTS

SKIN

PELVIC FINS

BODY

DORSAL FIN

B. CROSS SECTION SHOWING THE FIN ROOTS DISSECTED OUT

Fig. 15

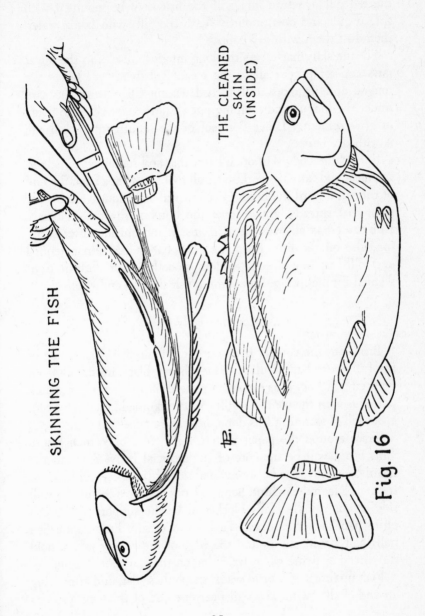

SKINNING THE FISH

THE CLEANED
SKIN
(INSIDE)

Fig. 16

31

the red gill structure intact, if the fish is to be mounted with spread gills and open mouth. Wash the gills with borax water, then dust them with dry borax.

Slit the skin that covers the long interior muscles in the lower jaws and scrape out all of the meat. Rub borax in. Leave the tongue and its roots undisturbed, except for slitting the skin under the tongue and scraping out all fatty material. Rub borax in after scraping. Leave the roof of the mouth intact and rub it with dry borax.

Spread the body skin open like a mat and scrape off all adhering meat and fatty tissue. Use a dull tool and scrape from the end of the tail toward the head. Give especial attention to removal of meat that spreads fanwise over the butts of the tail-fin bones. Rub dry borax all over the skin, inside and outside, after scraping, also on the fins. Keep the borax-cured fish skin extended and rolled up in a piece of oilcloth, smooth side of cloth in, until wanted for mounting. Never roll a fish skin up endwise.

Making the body form

Bring out the contact body outlines of the fish. Just inside of the full-figure body outline draw a heavy black inline. Cut out on the black line, thus making a pattern for the mannikin. Compare this with the contact outline of the skinned body. If a good, clean job of skinning was done, little difference will show.

Trace around the paper pattern on a piece of ½-inch board. This board will be the core of the artificial body. Saw out the board core. Check to be sure which side of the core-board will be the wall side in the mount. Screw a block of pine wood on the wall side, at the middle. This block will be the support of the fish on its panel when finished. Tack a row of slim little flat-headed nails halfway in, all around the edge of the core-board, to hold the thread or twine when wrapping on the excelsior "filling."

Pick up fine excelsior in wads, shape these flat, and after tying an end of the twine to a nail near one end of the core, proceed

32

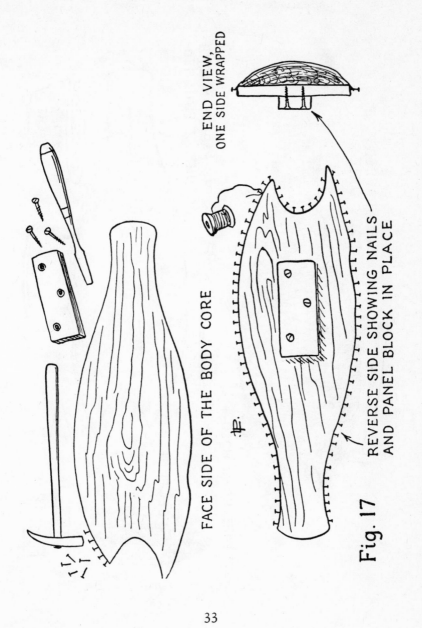

END VIEW,
ONE SIDE WRAPPED

FACE SIDE OF THE BODY CORE

REVERSE SIDE SHOWING NAILS
AND PANEL BLOCK IN PLACE

Fig. 17

33

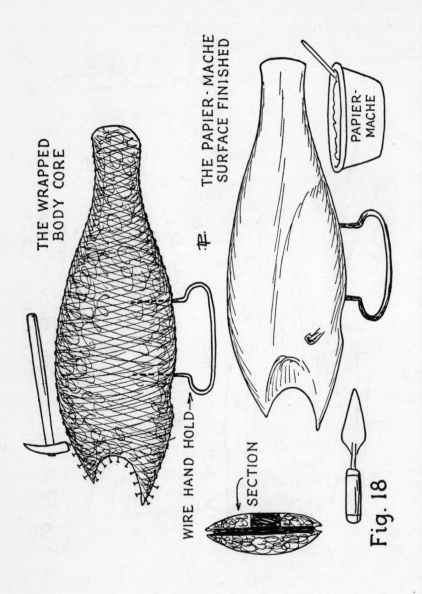

THE WRAPPED
BODY CORE

THE PAPIER-MACHE
SURFACE FINISHED

WIRE HAND HOLD→

PAPIER-MACHE

SECTION

Fig. 18

34

to wrap on one side of the body at a time. Keep it a little smaller than the actual dimensions. Consult the diameter measurements here, and keep within them. Loop the thread or twine back and forth from the edge of the belly line to the edge of the back line, drawing tightly as you proceed, thus making a neat, smooth excelsior body. When *both* sides are wrapped, drive the nails in snugly. Make a U-shaped wire handle with both ends sharpened. Set this in the belly of the form for holding it while you apply the papier-mâché surfacing over the excelsior, using a small trowel or a plaster tool. Work the papier-mâché into the excelsior. Model the surface to the natural shape of the real body, leaving grooves in the right places for the fins. Hang up by the wire handhold. Allow to dry, then work the surface smooth with a wood-file. When entirely dried, apply one coat of medium thin shellac.

Mounting

The fish skin may be pasted to the mannikin or put on without any adhesive. Use casein glue extended with flour paste if a pasted job is desired.

Wash the fish skin in borax saturate solution. Drain, then wipe it with a rag, inside and out. Brush paste all over inside of the body and tail. Lay the mannikin in the skin and fit the fin roots into their sockets. If the roots are too long, trim them to fit the sockets. Press the fish skin lightly into contact with the form. Push air bubbles out sidewise. The skin should not be punctured.

Sew up the body incision, beginning at the tail end. A sharp three-cornered needle is best for fish-skin sewing. Rub the thread with shoemakers' wax or petroleum wax. Seat the skull and throat on the two points at the front end of the form. Turn the fish over on a wire-cloth rack, and stuff the cheeks carefully with fine excelsior.

Prop the jaws open with a piece of balsa wood or a wrapped ball of excelsior. Pin the ends of the upper and lower jaws to the

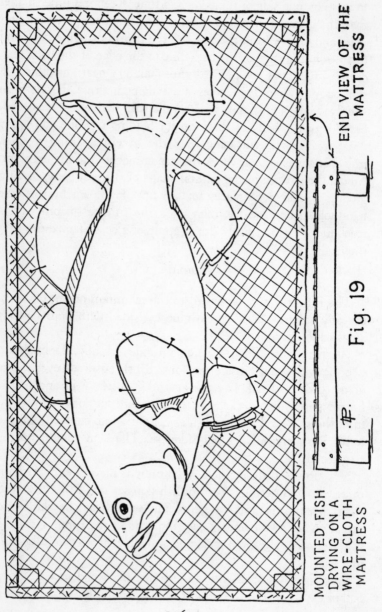

MOUNTED FISH
DRYING ON A
WIRE-CLOTH
MATTRESS

END VIEW OF THE
MATTRESS

Fig. 19

block. Raise the gill cover on the view side of the fish, blocking it open, same as the mouth. Pin the gill cover to the block. Comb the red gills, dust them with borax, then re-comb them. Prop the gill bars apart, spaced evenly, with pieces of cardboard. Adjust them carefully.

Keep the fins from drying by dampening them with borax water while working on the remainder of the fish. Dampen and card the marginal membrane of the gill cover. Cut two curved strips of light cardboard between which to pin the membrane.

Spread and card the fins. Lay wads of cotton under the gill cover and the fins to support the carding until all are dry. Check the mount for defects. Feel over the entire fish with the fingers for bumps and hollows that might mar the appearance of the surface. Adjust the tongue and block it into position. Allow the fish plenty of time to dry.

Retouching and coloring

Set a glass eye in the show side of the fish with a papier-mâché lining in the eye socket.

Make modeling wax by melting yellow petroleum wax in a double cooker, removing from the stove, and adding a small amount of turpentine, stirring it well. Color the wax white with tube oil color stirred in while the wax is hot. Paint the hot wax into cotton laid in the mouth parts, then model it into shape when cooled.

Remove the gill and fin cards. Add a backing of Scotch tape on the gill-cover margin and the fins, one layer on the gill edge, two on backs of the fins. Apply talcum powder or whiting to any sticky parts of the Scotch tape that are left exposed. Trim the edges neatly without cutting off any of the fin structure. Any tears in the fins may be patched with the Scotch tape, applied on the reverse side.

Give the fish skin and fronts of the fins one thin, even coat of shellac. Allow this to dry completely.

HALVED NATURAL BRANCH FRAME

A NOVEL VENEER PANEL IDEA

Fig. 20

38

Use tube oil colors, refined linseed oil, and turpentine for painting the colors and pattern on the fish. The color tints are first brushed on, then carefully stippled and blended and allowed to dry. The dusky markings are then brushed on and stippled over the base-color tints. Flat-bristle brushes are best for this work. Small red sable brushes are used for the fine details.

A pearly fish's coloring is simulated by giving the whole fish several coats of pearl essence in liquid celluloid. Six coats or more of the pearl are required to give the natural-looking undercoat an even appearance. The celluloid dries rapidly so that the "pearl" coat may be done in a day's time. The colors and pattern painting are then put on as described above.

For pearl-coloring muskies, a little "ex ex" brilliant (commercial description), aluminum powder may be added to the transparent raw umber coloring of the back and sides. When skillfully mixed, this combination has a natural bronzy appearance.

When buying tube oil colors for fish coloring, select colors of as translucent a nature as possible, and all of assured permanence. Good color makers have a select list of known permanent colors from which to draw your stock.

The mounted fish may be hung directly on a wall or it may be mounted on a shield. Either way is satisfactory. Framed, stained plywood panels make good lightweight backgrounds for mounted fish.

PART TWO

MOUNTING A HARD-SCALED FISH BY THE "SAND-FILL" METHOD

For mounting by this method the fish skin is prepared in the same way as described in Part One.

Sew the long incision toward the center from both ends, leaving an opening large enough to pour dry sand through to fill the skin completely. Stuff a plug of rags into the shoulder girdle to hold the sand filling in place. After placing the filling of sand, sew up the remainder of the incision.

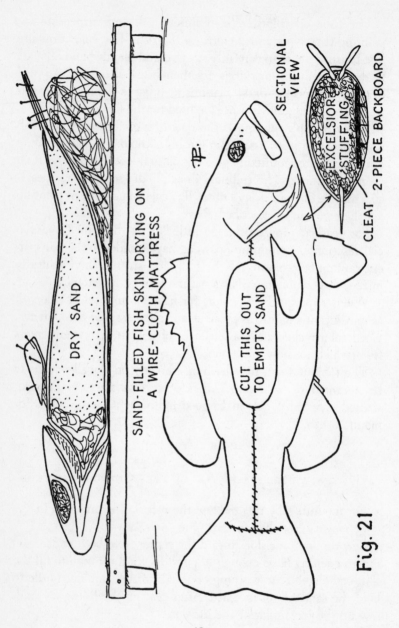

DRY SAND

SAND-FILLED FISH SKIN DRYING ON
A WIRE-CLOTH MATTRESS

CUT THIS OUT
TO EMPTY SAND

SECTIONAL
VIEW

EXCELSIOR
STUFFING

CLEAT 2-PIECE BACKBOARD

Fig. 21

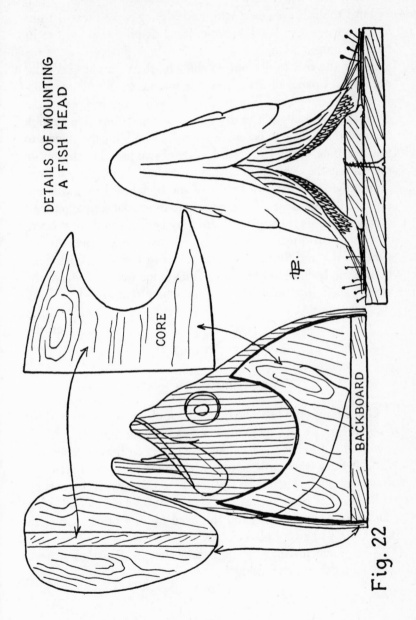

DETAILS OF MOUNTING
A FISH HEAD

CORE

BACKBOARD

Fig. 22

41

Turn the fish over on a wire-cloth drying-rack. Treat the fins and head details as in Part One, after shaping the body to its natural conformation.

Allow the fish to dry out completely, then turn it over. Cut out an oval panel of skin from the middle of the incised side. Pour and scrape out all of the sand. Shellac the interior of the dried skin, and allow it to dry out. (This means to give enough time for the shellac to become entirely hard.) Stuff the skin with fine excelsior. Cut a back-board made of two pieces to slip inside the skin at the oval opening. Lay two cleats in on the excelsior filling, then slip the two halves of the back-board in and screw them fast to the cleats. Tack the skin to the back-board all around the oval opening. The back-board may be fitted with hangers to place the fish directly on a wall, or it may be screwed upon a panel. Color and finish the same way as in Part One. Fish done by this method are light weight. When mounted on framed plywood panels they may be hung anywhere that an oil painting could be hung.

PART THREE

MOUNTING A FISH HEAD

Cut through the fish's body just back of the shoulders and include the breast fins, when removing a head for mounting. Make a contact outline of the head and shoulders on brown paper, the same as for a whole fish mount. Measure vertical and horizontal diameters of the shoulders and jot these down with the sketch.

Prepare the head in the same way as for a whole mount. After the borax-curing is done, roll the head up in a piece of oilcloth and keep it in a cool place.

The accompanying drawings show details of making a head and shoulder fish mounting.

CHAPTER IV

PREPARING AND MOUNTING A BIRD

In this chapter a quail will be our selection for mounting, for such a bird is compact and easy to prepare, making a handsome trophy when well finished. In its small way it is physically representative of all our native American game birds. All of the species, whether large or small, are a delight for the taxidermist to prepare and mount. Their skins are generally tough and durable, and their fat is of such a nature as to be easily removed. When a good specimen is shot, handle it carefully. Plug the shot holes, mouth, and vent with cotton applied with a sharpened twig, then roll the bird in paper, and carry it carefully.

Lay the bird on a piece of brown paper and make contact outlines from several poses before skinning. Sketch in the outlines of the distinct feather tracts, such as the neck cape, the shoulder coverts or scapulars, the rump, the wing plumage areas, and the flank and breast masses. Such studies are useful in the work of assembling and mounting a bird. Take a little time and do them well.

After the bird is skinned, add side and top view contact outlines of the carcass and neck to the page of sketches. Spot in the shoulder, hip, knee, and tail joints. Take note that the tail quills do not set snugly against the rump, but are located on a well-defined caudal appendage or tail. After a side view of the body is made, draw a pear-shaped outline with blue pencil around just outside of the natural outline. This will be your pattern for the artificial body.

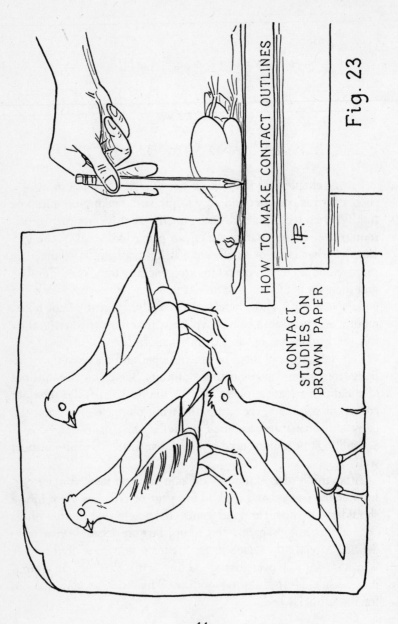

HOW TO MAKE CONTACT OUTLINES

CONTACT STUDIES ON BROWN PAPER

Fig. 23

44

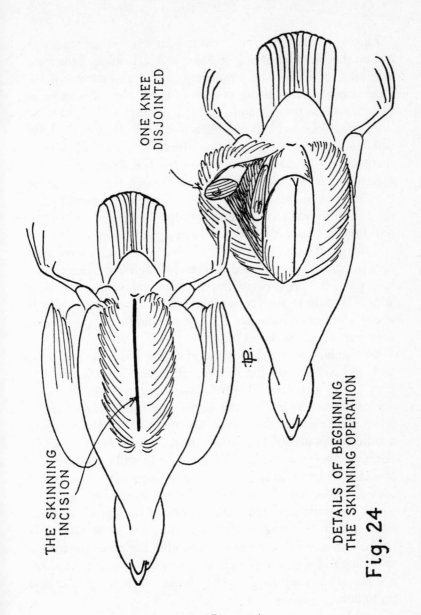

THE SKINNING
INCISION

ONE KNEE
DISJOINTED

DETAILS OF BEGINNING
THE SKINNING OPERATION

Fig. 24

45

Lay the bird on the table, head to your left. Have a supply of cornmeal at hand for drying up blood and body juices if the meat is wanted for eating. Use powdered borax for this purpose if the meat is not wanted. If not previously done, plug all shot holes and the mouth, nostrils, and vent with cotton.

Part the belly and breast feathers along the center of the body where a bare strip of skin shows plainly on most birds. Use a sharp scalpel in making an incision the full length of the abdomen and breast. Cut carefully just through the skin, leaving the abdominal wall intact. The skin and belly wall are easily separated. Use the thumb-nails and a scalpel handle in peeling the skin from the body. After the incision is made, start at the front end and pry the skin free from the breast meat. Sprinkle on cornmeal or borax as you proceed. When the thigh is exposed on one side, push the leg forward inside of the cut so that the knee joint is brought to view. Sever the knee with a cartilage knife or scissors. Repeat on the other leg. Use care not to cut the skin on the other side of the knees.

Set the bird up on the front end of the body. Bend the tail back and cut through the rectum, tail meat, and bone just forward of the quill butts. Be careful not to cut the skin on top of the tail. Continue holding the bird up on the front end of the breast. Peel the skin down over the hips, back, and sides, using a knife where needed to cut the skin free. Some birds are easily skinned, others not. When the body is fairly well uncovered, the bird may be hung up to advantage on a chain-and-hooks, so that both of the worker's hands are free for the job of skinning.

A home-made set of chain-and-hooks may be rigged from three short strands of strong, small-gauge chain and three large fishhooks with the barbs removed. Assemble the three units on a split ring, and with a piece of twine, hang at any height required. Set the hooks deep in the pelvis bones when hanging a bird up to finish skinning.

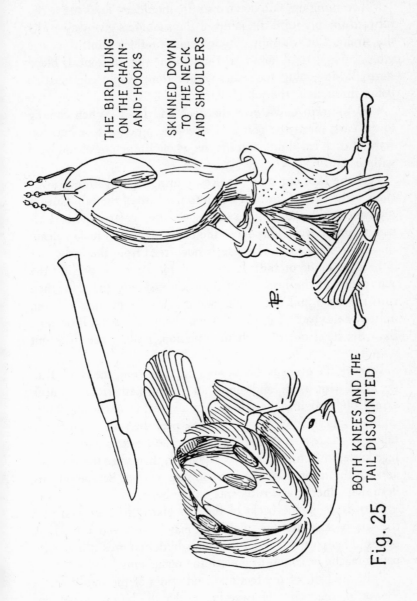

THE BIRD HUNG ON THE CHAIN-AND-HOOKS

SKINNED DOWN TO THE NECK AND SHOULDERS

BOTH KNEES AND THE TAIL DISJOINTED

Fig. 25

47

When hung up, skin down over the shoulders. Press the wings forward sharply until the joints of the shoulders give way under the strain. Cut carefully through one shoulder joint, then the other, being careful not to cut through the skin in front. If blood starts flowing, plug the veins with cotton. Apply cornmeal or borax throughout the job of skinning.

Peel the skin down over the neck and head. When coming to the ears, insert the points of tweezers, pinched together, forward of each ear lining and lift the whole lining out of the head without cutting.

Peel the face out over the eyes, cutting the lid linings away close to the skull. Continue down to the base of the bill. Cut off the base of the skull with a cartilage knife, leaving the base attached to the neck. This opens the brain cavity and makes cleaning of the skull easy. The skin is now freed from the body.

If some kinds of birds have heads too large for peeling the skin over, cut the neck off at the body inside of the skin, then turn the head and neck right side out. Make an incision from on top of the back of the head down along the neck a little way. Skin the head out through this incision, pulling the neck out with it.

Remove the eyeballs, brain, and jaw meat from the skull. Rub the skull with borax, and scrape all fat and flesh from the neck skin. Rub borax into the skin. Clean all meat from the leg, wing, and tail bones. To clean out the legs, peel the skin down to the top of the bare part of the legs. Sever the tendons with a cartilage knife, in front and back of the bone, then seize the cut ends and rip the meat from the bone in one motion. Scrape off any flesh that adheres, and rub borax on the bones.

In owls, open the backs of the legs above the feet, and peel the skin back so that the thick meat may be removed around the bones. This part of the legs in such birds requires filling with papier-mâché or cotton to replace the tarsus muscles.

Split the balls of the feet and undersides of the toes. Force a skewer, or the points of tweezers, under the bunch of tendons just back of the balls of the feet, and pull the tendons out of the backs of the legs above the feet. Cut them off in the balls of the feet. Do this only after the meat of the drumsticks has been removed. Scrape and shear fatty tissue out of the balls of the feet and undersides of the toes.

Peel the skin of the wings down to the elbows. Cut the tendons through just above the elbows, and strip the meat from the upper arm bones.

The forearm meat may be removed by pushing the skin down over the fronts of the forearms in short-winged birds. Long-winged birds require a forearm incision to be made in the bare strip of skin along the middle of the underside. The hand bones also should be incised and have the meat cleaned out of them. Rub borax into all parts as you proceed. Cut the forearm muscles free at the elbows and strip them out down to the wrists, then cut off there. Do not sever the large flight quills from the forearm bones.

If fat is not included in the skin structure, it may be scraped off readily. Apply borax, and re-scrape until all fat is gone. Waterfowl have fat in the skin layers which requires careful shearing out, then a thorough scraping, and finally a washing to remove the grease. In the shearing process it is important to use care not to shear the feather butts off with the inner skin layer that encloses the fat. When scraping a greasy bird skin, always work from the tail toward the head.

Wash bloodstains out of the plumage with weak ammonia water, using a soft sponge or piece of rag to work with. Soap and borax-water washing is good for all bird skins, followed by soaking and rinsing in borax saturate solution. Squeeze the skin out of this, press the remainder of the moisture out of the skin and plumage with clean cloths, then dust and fluff in powdered borax. Borax for this purpose may be purchased at a saving by the hundred-pound sack, direct from the producer.

Following the above treatment, bird skins are ready for immediate mounting, or they may be dried and stored for future

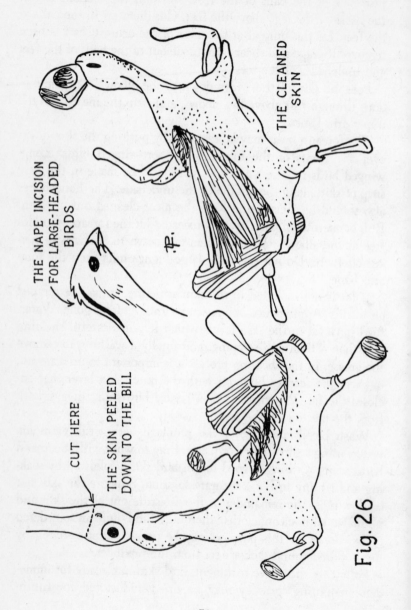

THE NAPE INCISION
FOR LARGE-HEADED
BIRDS

THE CLEANED
SKIN

CUT HERE

THE SKIN PEELED
DOWN TO THE BILL

Fig. 26

mounting. If a bird skin is to be mounted at once, moisten it all over inside with borax solution, then roll it up in a piece of oil-cloth until the artificial body and the wires are prepared.

Dried skins are relaxed by brushing them inside with borax solution when about ready to be mounted. Relax the feet a day or so ahead of the body skin, by wrapping them in borax-dampened cloths.

The best beating-brush for knocking dust out of plumage after dusting and fluffing, is made from the hairy tip of an ox-tail. Skin the tip of the tail. Borax-cure the hide and nail it to a handle made from a piece of broomstick tapered to a point.

Mounting the bird

The first step in mounting a bird skin is to turn the neck and head inside out and stuff the eye sockets level full of soft excelsior. Then wrap a layer of cotton over the top of the skull, down over each side, and tuck its margin in under the jaws. Turn the head back into the skin, being sure to stuff the front edge of the cotton layer down close to the base of the bill.

The second step is the making of the artificial body. No better material than clean excelsior has been found for this purpose. Fine jewelers' excelsior is best for small birds; ordinary excelsior is suitable for large ones. For all types of birds having robust bodies, the pear-, or egg-shaped artificial body is recommended. This shape, when properly made and installed, requires little or no loose filling to be placed after the skin is on it. The strictly natural-shaped artificial body is a disappointing affair on which to assemble a bird skin. Loose filling is not always easily placed. For flat-bodied birds, such as rails, herons, etc., the pear-shaped silhouette is used, but with the sides flattened somewhat.

To start making the bird body, wrap a handful of excelsior into a club shape, more or less pointed at both ends. Fold this in the middle and wrap it together firmly to make an ovate body core. When through with any stage of excelsior wrapping, cut

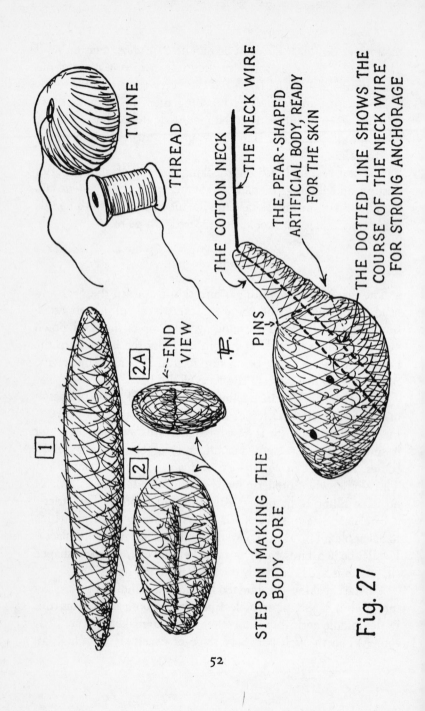

TWINE

THREAD

THE COTTON NECK

THE NECK WIRE

THE PEAR-SHAPED
ARTIFICIAL BODY, READY
FOR THE SKIN

THE DOTTED LINE SHOWS THE
COURSE OF THE NECK WIRE
FOR STRONG ANCHORAGE

1

2

2A — END
VIEW

PINS

STEPS IN MAKING THE
BODY CORE

Fig. 27

the thread or twine, tuck its end through the excelsior with the tweezers, and pull it up snugly. Around the body core, wrap flat wads of excelsior, continuing with this work until the pear-shaped form is attained. When this is held over the contact sketch of the real body, it will approximate its dimensions according to the side-view drawing and the pencil outline.

The third step is to cut and sharpen the neck, leg, wing, and tail wires, also to make several small pointed wires to hold cops wrapping on the plumage when the bird is set up and the feathers are adjusted. The wires for supporting the neck and legs should be strong enough so that there will be no wobbling of the finished mount. Annealed, galvanized iron wire is most practical. Cut the neck wire two and one-half times the length of the body form, and sharpen it at both ends. Cut the two leg wires two and one-half times the length of a leg, from the knee to the ball of the foot; sharpen these at one end only. Cut the two wing wires twice the length of the wing from the shoulder joint to the end of the hand bones, and sharpen both ends. Cut the tail wire one and one-half times the length of the body. Sharpen one end of it, and bend the other end into a T shape for supporting the tail quills. Cut eight feather-wrapping supports from small-gauge wire, each 4 inches long (longer for large birds), sharpen them at one end, and bend the other end into an N shape.

Before inserting the neck wire in the body, determine the pose that the mount is to have. If the head is to be held high, make a spot with ink at a point above the center of the front end of the body. If the head is to be held low, put the ink spot at the center of the front. Push the neck wire in at the ink spot and through the body lengthwise. Turn back the protruding end of the wire, and clinch it into the body.

Spin a cotton neck upon the wire in front of the body, twirling the first layers of cotton tight and smooth. The remainder of the layers may be slightly looser, but they should be placed carefully and smoothly. Large bird necks may be made with excelsior cores wrapped down with thread, then finished with a cotton surface.

53

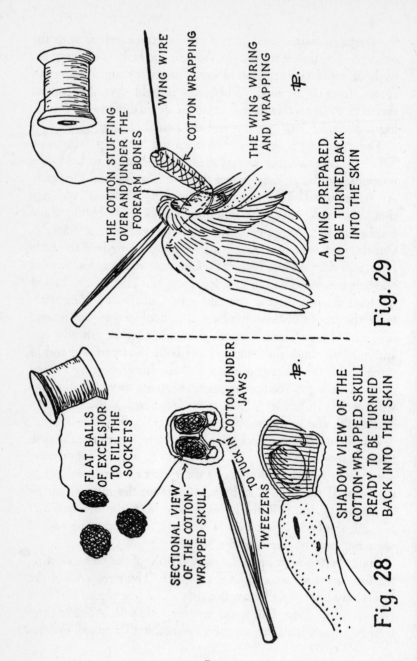

WING WIRE

COTTON WRAPPING

THE COTTON STUFFING OVER AND/UNDER THE FOREARM BONES

THE WING WIRING AND WRAPPING

A WING PREPARED TO BE TURNED BACK INTO THE SKIN

Fig. 29

FLAT BALLS OF EXCELSIOR TO FILL THE SOCKETS

SECTIONAL VIEW OF THE COTTON-WRAPPED SKULL

TO TUCK IN COTTON UNDER JAWS

TWEEZERS

SHADOW VIEW OF THE COTTON-WRAPPED SKULL READY TO BE TURNED BACK INTO THE SKIN

Fig. 28

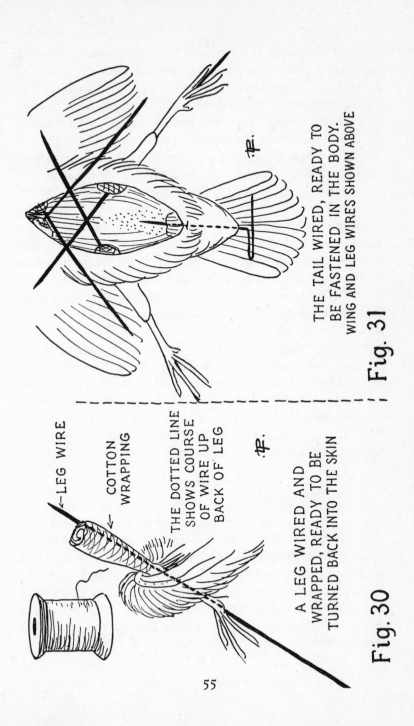

LEG WIRE

COTTON
WRAPPING

THE DOTTED LINE
SHOWS COURSE
OF WIRE UP
BACK OF LEG

A LEG WIRED AND
WRAPPED, READY TO BE
TURNED BACK INTO THE SKIN

Fig. 30

THE TAIL WIRED, READY TO
BE FASTENED IN THE BODY.
WING AND LEG WIRES SHOWN ABOVE

Fig. 31

Wrap all outer layers of necks with thread. Taper the cotton neck and make it just a little fuller than the real neck. At the top of the neck add on just enough more to seat in the brain cavity. Pin the first wrapped neck layer to the body to prevent the neck from slipping on the wire. Taper the base of the neck a little out on the body, and pin the last layer in several places on the front of the body to hold it snugly in position. Mark the shoulder joints, knee joints, and tail attachment on the body with ink spots.

Wire the wing bones by slipping the wire along the back of the elbow joint. Probe one point of the wire out into the wing tip, through the cords under the wrist. Wrap the wire to the upper arm bone with thread. Replace the muscle shape with cotton smoothly wrapped over the bone. Stuff the forearm with cotton, and neatly sew up the incision. Repeat on the other wing. Bend the wings half-closed. A round needle is best for average bird-skin sewing, but use a three-cornered needle on tough-skinned specimens.

Slip a leg wire up through the back of a leg until the tip of the wire is just beyond the top of the bone at the knee. Wrap the wire to the bone with a few turns of thread. Replace the leg muscles with a tapered wrapping of cotton. Bind this with a few turns of thread. The wire should slip freely to go through the body. Repeat on the other leg. Put the tail wire in through the tail on its underside.

Assembling the bird

To assemble the bird, begin by wrapping a little cotton over the tip of the neck wire so that it will pass inside of the neck skin without catching into it. Push the tip of the wire out through the mouth, remove the cotton, then draw the wire back and run its sharp end through the opening in the back of the skull, then through between the eye sockets and out through the roof of the mouth. Curve the wire a little downward at its tip so that it will be more easily passed out through the roof of the mouth. Push the brain cavity on the end of the neck.

56

Fig. 32

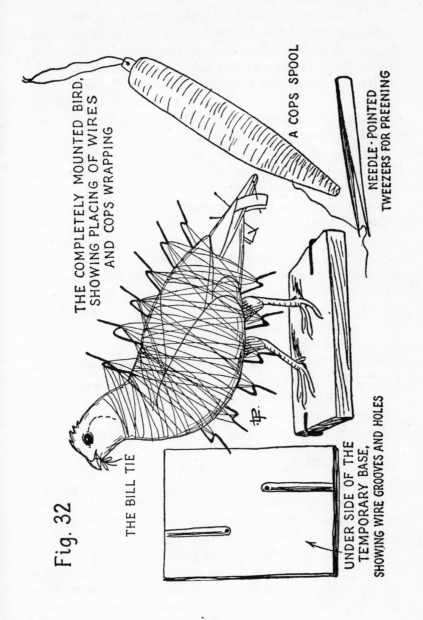

THE COMPLETELY MOUNTED BIRD, SHOWING PLACING OF WIRES AND COPS WRAPPING

A COPS SPOOL

NEEDLE-POINTED TWEEZERS FOR PREENING

THE BILL TIE

UNDER SIDE OF THE TEMPORARY BASE, SHOWING WIRE GROOVES AND HOLES

Draw the skin down over the neck. Pass the wing wire ends through the body at their ink marks, then clinch them into opposite sides of the body. Pull the body skin partly into place and pass the leg wire on one side into the ink mark at the knee. Work the leg back on its wire repeatedly, and feed the wire through the body until enough of it comes out on the other side to be turned and clinched into the body. Push the knee down to the body. Repeat with the other leg.

Push the tail wire in at its ink mark. Stuff the tail with cotton and settle the tail to the body, then push the wire in until the T bend rests near the skin under the large quills, but not close enough to press the feather butts apart.

Bend the legs somewhat backward along the body. Pick the bird up by its legs and shake it a little to loosen the feathers so that they will settle into place readily. Sew up the long breast incision. Bring the legs back, then down to the standing position. Drill the base or perch and place the bird upon it, temporarily bending the leg wires around from underneath, to hold the feet close if on a perch. Avoid pulling the feet down so tightly that they are too flat-heeled.

Lift the wings a little and adjust the body skin under them, pinning it up in place at the arm-pits. If the head was skinned out through a nape incision, sew this up. Where necessary, moisten the skin before sewing, using borax-water.

Bend the wings, neck, legs, and tail to suit the pose chosen, then, with tweezers, preen the plumage to its natural effect. Study the feather tracts, noting how they overlie each other like the shingles on a roof.

Begin the feather dressing at the tail. Spread or close the tail quills as desired, and card them crosswise above and below with thin card strips held together with three or four pins stuck through from top to bottom. The quill bases should lie neatly on top of the T bend of the tail wire, which is to be given a curved shape under the quills before the carding is done. Next dress the rump and back plumage, then the large breast masses

58

on each side, then the wings and shoulder coverts and lastly the shoulder cape, neck, and head.

When all of the plumage is finished, set the glass eyes in place with a little papier-mâché in the eye sockets, adjusting the lids with a needle point. Cut off the tip of the neck wire and bend back the remaining end flat in the roof of the mouth. Tie the bill shut with a loop of thread sewn through the nostrils, first placing a little cotton in the throat. Pin the toes in place on the perch or base, using insect pins if possible. (Small needles are better than common pins for this purpose, in a pinch.)

If spread wings are desired, the flight quills are to be carded with long strips of thin pasteboard pinned across them, then supported on rolls of cotton held up with sharpened wires set into the sides of the body.

The feet of large birds need to have some papier-mâché filling in the toes and soles, with the incisions being carefully sewn up. With the bird well shaped and preened, push a row of the N-tipped wires in along the center of the back and another row along the center of the breast. Tie an end of cotton cops to one of the front back wires, then loosely bind the plumage from front to rear with the cops thread. One side may be done at a time.

Give the specimen another checking over, then set it away to dry. Give it an occasional check-up while drying. When perfectly dry, replace the tints of bare skin, bill, and feet, with tube oil colors, linseed oil, and turpentine. Straighten the ends of the leg wires, cut off some surplus, and clinch the remaining end of each wire into the perch or base where it will not show. Cut away the cops feather wrapping, and draw out the N-tipped wires with a twisting motion. Preen the feathers again, and the bird is ready for showing.

Old dried bird skins should be softened in preparation for mounting by having all of their temporary stuffing removed and replaced with cloths dampened in borax solution. Wrap such a skin in oilcloth and lay it overnight in a cool place. If there is any doubt about the freshness of the skin when it was dried, weak carbolic water should replace the borax solution for the purpose of relaxing the skin. Do not use carbolic acid, alcohol, or formalin with borax solution. The feet need to be previously wrapped in cloths wet with the solution, as they are the hardest part of the bird skin to relax.

When the skin is relaxed enough to be turned inside out, scrape it and treat it from then on as described for handling a fresh bird skin. Arsenically "cured" skins should be shunned by any young taxidermist who values his health, for such skins, carelessly handled, have produced many casualties and numerous cripples.

To make a "cabinet" skin for study purposes, prepare the skin as for mounting. Wrap the skull, leg, and wing bones with cotton. Make an ovate, rather flattened artificial body with a wire and cotton neck. Insert the body, and sew up the skin. Take one stitch through the wings at the elbows and through the back; with this tie the wings in place. Push the cotton-wrapped leg bones well up into the sides, leaving only the bare tarsi exposed outside of the plumage.

Wire the tail to the body. Tie the feet together with the data label string. Adjust the plumage, and stuff the eye sockets and throat with cotton. Tie the bill shut, and rest the bird on its back in a curved piece of wire-cloth to dry.

To sex a bird, slit through the ribs on one side, and look for the testes or ovaries near the front end of the pelvis.

CHAPTER V

PREPARING AND MOUNTING A WILDCAT

Most mammal skins are readily handled for mounting. By using the correct processes and remembering that a mammal skin will not stand quite the stresses that a bird skin will, the taxidermist can expect marked success in preparing furry trophies for both rugs and full mounts. Our native mammalian fauna still provides ample material. The method here described may be applied with equal success on a raccoon or a caribou.

Refer to the text drawings for details of the removal of a whole mammal skin.

A complete skin should go through the same treatment of double salting and then being processed by a competent taxidermy tanner, as is described for deer scalps. Raw skins should not be considered for mounting, except in the case of small mammals, birds, fishes, and reptiles.

The easiest larger mammal mountings to make are done with either flat skins or skins removed by means of the full-length dorsal incision. If the flat style of skin is used, of course there is plenty of sewing to be done when assembling the skin on the body form, but this should not be irksome to one handy with needle and thread. Mounting a round-type skin is beyond the amateur's ability.

If the dorsal incision, from back of head to tip of tail, is used, the legs are skinned with only the soles of the feet and wrists and ankles incised. This style of skin is drawn on the body form from underneath, as a glove is pulled over the hand. There is

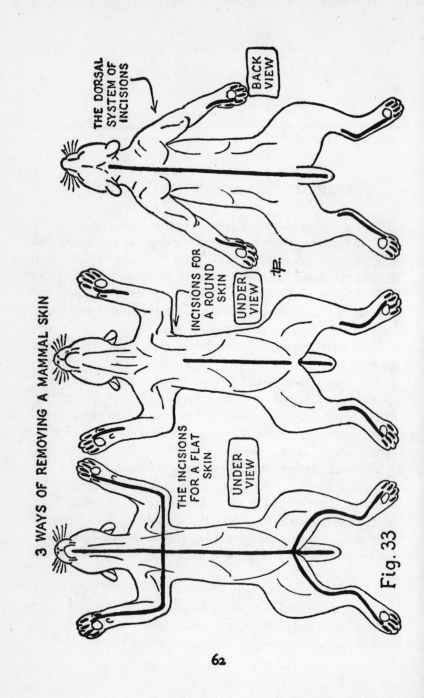

3 WAYS OF REMOVING A MAMMAL SKIN

THE DORSAL
SYSTEM OF
INCISIONS

BACK VIEW

INCISIONS FOR
A ROUND SKIN

UNDER VIEW

THE INCISIONS FOR A FLAT
SKIN

UNDER VIEW

Fig. 33

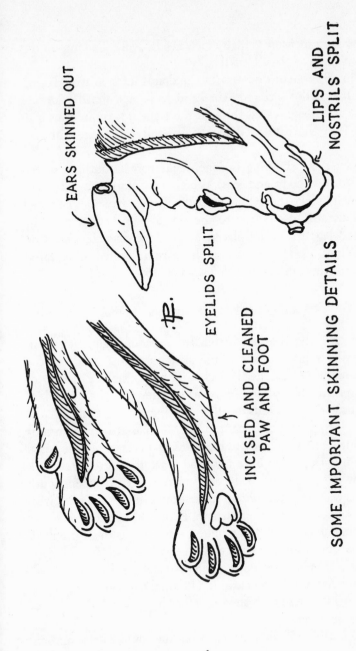

EARS SKINNED OUT

LIPS AND
NOSTRILS SPLIT

EYELIDS SPLIT

INCISED AND CLEANED
PAW AND FOOT

SOME IMPORTANT SKINNING DETAILS

Fig. 34

63

but one long incision to give much needle work. Sewing up the paws and feet are small matters.

All in all, a mount done with the dorsal incision would seem preferable, if the specimen comes to hand not already skinned out flat or fur-skin cased through the standard, rump cross-incision. Clean the skull and leg bones, and rub them with dry borax.

However the skinning is done, make contact outlines of the entire skinned body and legs. When rigor mortis is past is the best time to make the drawings, as the carcass may then be posed in various attitudes. Measure the side-to-side diameters of the body and legs in several places. Mark these diameters as cross-topped lines out at the sides of the parts indicated. Circumference measurements are of little use in constructing a form.

Making the body form or mannikin

After choosing the best sketch from among the contact outlines, make a heavy black inline all around just inside of the natural outline of the head, neck, and body. Make a tracing of the figure thus black-lined to use as a pattern for the mannikin.

Cleat some pine boards together, making an area of them large enough to cover the body pattern. Lay the pattern on the boards thus joined, and mark around the pattern; then saw out the board core. If it is desired to have the head separate and set on a neck rod, saw the head and body out separately. If an open-mouth mount is wanted, either set up the natural skull on the form with the jaws fixed open with plaster-of-Paris and cut rope fiber, or use a commercial head with tongue, gums, and teeth all installed. Old rope, cut in short lengths and plucked out, will furnish good fiber filler for plaster-of-Paris. If the natural skull is to be used, boil it in borax-water and clean it. (Natural teeth are apt to crack in time, while those furnished in paper head forms are made of indestructible material.)

Trace outlines of the four legs from the contact drawings and

64

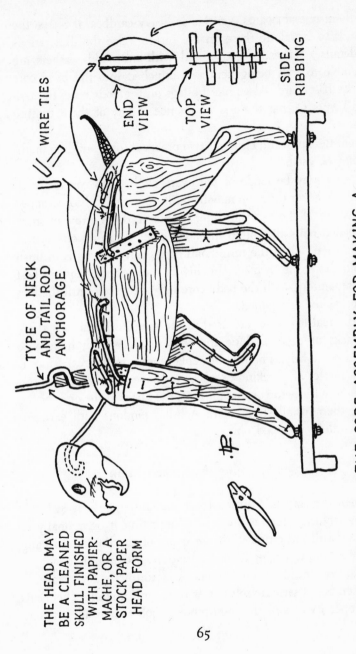

WIRE TIES

TYPE OF NECK
AND TAIL ROD
ANCHORAGE

THE HEAD MAY
BE A CLEANED
SKULL FINISHED
WITH PAPIER-
MACHE, OR A
STOCK PAPER
HEAD FORM

END
VIEW

TOP
VIEW

SIDE
RIBBING

THE CORE ASSEMBLY FOR MAKING A
DIRECT-BUILT MAMMAL MANNIKIN

Fig.35

saw them out of boards, veneer, or heavy cardboard. Shape the leg rods to lay along these on the inside. (See the illustrations for details.) Threaded rods fitted with nuts and washers are preferable to rods being bent and clinched into the body core and the baseboard. Assemble the legs on the body core, tightening all nuts so that there is no chance of any of them coming loose.

From here onward, either of two practical form-building methods may be used.

A shell may be made of hardware cloth, then covered with papier-mâché, or the form may be built up with excelsior wrapped with twine. If the excelsior filler is chosen, drive a row of small flat-headed nails all around the body core. Wrap up one side at a time; then, when the form is all done, drive the nails in flush to hold the twine in place. In this kind of job the legs are best done separately, with the body core left uncovered until the legs are completed and joined.

If the real leg bones are used in the mount, fit the rods along the backs of them and tie the rods in place with light wire twisted on tightly. The muscle replacement on the real bones is then a matter of plucking excelsior to shape and wrapping it on the bones with twine or thread. Drill the hocks at the ends of the bones, then install strong wire Achilles tendons with excelsior muscle-filling wrapped on.

Mothproofing the leathered skin

When the skin is returned from the tanner, soak it in borax saturate solution for an hour or so, agitating it occasionally to speed up full saturation. Squeeze it out of the liquid and hang it over a pole to drain. It may be mounted damp or it may be fully fluffed and dried for immediate mounting or for storage.

When borax saturate solution is used with no other chemicals to hamper its action, the mothproofing job that results is complete and permanent. Dusting and fluffing the pelt in powdered borax is recommended following the borax-solution soaking.

When a boraxed skin is drying, it should be stretched and worked now and then until finally dried out.

A piece of rattan or dowel rod is handy for beating the dust out of a fluffed skin. Beat the borax out on a large piece of paper, to be returned to the dusting box.

Mounting

In preparing to mount the skin, make up a sufficient amount of casein glue and flour paste to complete the adjustment of the skin on the form, or use any reliable ready-prepared commercial skin paste, if this is made without arsenic.

The excelsior type of form may be used with or without a papier-mâché finished surface. Muscular detail work depends upon the sculpturing ability of the taxidermist. If the excelsior-built form is used, no pasting need be done, with the exception of the face.

When mounting a dorsal-incision job, unbolt the form from the base, then draw the skin over the legs and body, and tie the skin together on the back with several single stitches spaced a few inches apart.

Fill the feet with papier-mâché, shape them somewhat, sew up the foot incisions and re-bolt the animal on the base. Cut the temporary back ties loose on the neck. Paste the head and neck skin first, then cut the rest of the back ties, and brush and press some paste down inside of the legs. When these parts are pasted to the form, paste on one side of the body skin; repeat the operation on the other side.

Begin sewing the back incision at the rump end, leaving the tail until last. Draw the dorsal incision neatly together, with all pattern markings in the fur accurately adjusted. The paste will suffice to hold the skin now, so that no ties need be replaced. After sewing along a few inches from the rump, tie the thread and cut it off. Then go ahead and start another section of sewing at the mid-back, going along several inches; tie and cut the thread. Then start sewing at the base of the neck; complete this section of the incision up to its end on the back of the head. By sewing up parts of the long incision in this way, a better adjustment of the skin will result. If the skin on one side of the seam is longer than the other side anywhere, catch it up gradually by taking slightly longer stitches on the long side until the sides come out even. Begin at the end of the tail to sew it up. Tie the edges of the skin in a few places.

As you proceed, always keep the fur picked out of the stitches. Small stitches, with the fur consistently picked from inside of them, will result in a dorsal seam that will not show when the fur is combed and dressed over it. The dorsal-incision mount is practical for all long or medium-haired mammals, regardless of size.

If the flat type of skin is being mounted, the animal may be assembled and pasted completely before being unbolted from the base for sewing and finishing the detail work. When mounting a flat skin on the form, paste and adjust the head skin first, except around the eyes, ears, nose, and mouth. After pasting the head skin, wrap the head in borax-dampened cloths.

Using small nails, tack the body skin along the center of the neck and back of the form, to the root of the tail. Drive the nails only halfway in.

Pin a large piece of paper by its edge along the back outside of the skin, and allow the paper to hang over one side. Lift the other side of the skin and lay it over the paper, nicely spread for pasting. Brush paste evenly over the inside of this half of the body skin. Also spread an even layer of paste over the exposed half of the mannikin. Turn the pasted half of the skin down on the body, and mold it into place. Paste the leg skin and legs of the mannikin on that side, and adjust the skin on the legs. Draw the points of the body skin into place under the armpits and flanks.

Turn the paper over on the other side, and repeat. Unbolt the animal from the base and turn it on its back. A canvas hammock on a pair of joined X horses is handy to rest a mammal in while sewing it up, though it may be simply leaned, feet up, against a wall or any upright support.

Sew up the long body incision first, then the tail and legs. Before beginning the leg stitching at the feet, put in their papier-mâché filling.

After the incisions are sewn up with the markings on the fur accurately adjusted, re-bolt the specimen on its base and turn your attention to finishing the head details, to working air bubbles out from under the skin, and to shaping the feet and tail.

Paste the ear skins after slitting the inner skin under the upper or forward flange for inserting the ear liners. Beveled ear liners may be made of leather for a wildcat, a bear, or a wolf. Cut them after patterns of the real ear cartilages, and bevel them with a rasp. Moisten them with borax-water before pasting and inserting in the ears. Shape them inside of the ear skins. Use medium-thick leather, not heavy stock, but sufficient to retain their shape when dried and to support the ears perfectly. Seat them in papier-mâché butts of accurate natural size.

Paste around inside of the eyelid linings; set the eyes in papier-mâché, fill the lid linings to natural size, and adjust the lids with a darning-needle point. Paste the lips and nostrils, then fill them with papier-mâché and adjust, molding their details carefully.

If the work of mounting promises to be more than can be done in one day, wrap the feet and head in borax-dampened cloths and keep the animal in a cool place until the next day. Unwrap one extremity at a time and finish work on it before unwrapping another.

A framework of pine strips with cross-pieces screwed on its top for foot supports makes a handy temporary base on which to mount a specimen. The screwed cross-pieces may be moved to accommodate other mountings. Bore rod holes slightly larger than the rods used.

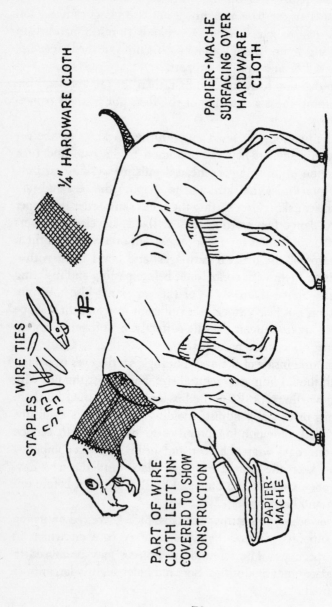

¼" HARDWARE CLOTH

PAPIER-MACHE SURFACING OVER HARDWARE CLOTH

STAPLES WIRE TIES

PART OF WIRE CLOTH LEFT UN-COVERED TO SHOW CONSTRUCTION

PAPIER-MACHE

NEARLY FINISHED MANNIKIN FOR A CAT

Fig. 36

Rod nuts should be nested in the compo of the bottoms of the feet of mammal mounts, to support the weight firmly on metal. Washers should be included both above and below the base. For the purpose of accommodating the installation of foot nuts, cut out a round section from the skin of the bottoms of the feet.

Whether the animal's mouth is to be open or closed, if the natural skull is cleaned and used, papier-mâché lips, nose, and facial details may be built on the face before assembling it on the mannikin. The skull should be mounted on a piece of rod plastered into the brain cavity, with the base of the skull sawed off. An artificial tongue and gums of colored wax and cotton may be built in after the mount is finished and dried. Composition tongues are sold by supply houses.

A good way to begin making a wax-finished tongue is to carve its general form, in smaller size, out of soft wood. Balsa wood is good for this purpose. This core is inserted between the lower jaws and fastened in with papier-mâché.

Melt wax in a double cooker and tint it with tube oil colors. A bit of cadmium red mixed into the wax will approximate the natural tongue color. Avoid making it too red; study natural tongues for color. Use a ½-inch flat bristle brush to apply the hot wax over the tongue core and the gums; then use a small metal plaster tool for modeling the surface to natural shape.

While the specimen is drying out, check over all facial and foot details occasionally, using a modeling tool to keep them in order until dry. When dry, comb and brush the fur all over. Color the end of the nose, the lips, and eyelids with oil paints, refined linseed oil, and turpentine. Mount the animal on its permanent base ready for showing.

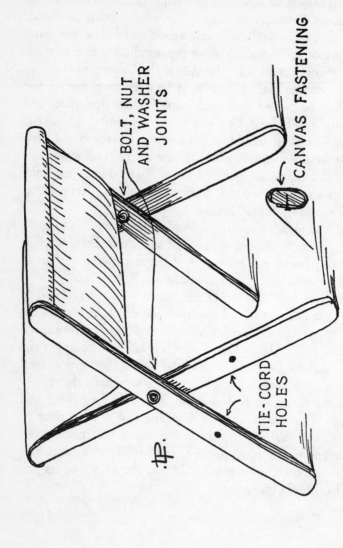

BOLT, NUT AND WASHER JOINTS

CANVAS FASTENING

TIE-CORD HOLES

ฮ.

Fig. 37

FRAME AND CANVAS HAMMOCK USED TO HOLD MOUNTED MAMMALS WHEN SEWING UP

CHAPTER VI

PREPARING AND MOUNTING A SMALL MAMMAL

A tough-skinned fox squirrel will furnish an ideal subject for consideration in this chapter.

An old squirrel has a skin of Herculean strength that makes a satisfying den trophy. When the taxidermist has succeeded in making a squirrel recognizable, he can sit back and congratulate himself, for there are more stuffed squirrels that defy identification than could be counted. But it should be a challenge to have on the workbench before you an animal that everyone knows.

Pose the dead squirrel on its side on a sheet of brown paper and make contact outlines of several attitudes. After skinning the specimen, make outlines of the carcass, posed like the superficial drawings. If the meat is wanted for food, use cornmeal to dry up body juices while skinning. If the meat is not wanted, use powdered borax.

Make an incision along the middle of the belly from in front of the vent up to the middle of the breast bone. Make an incision the full length of each palm and sole, continuing these for a little way up the backs of the wrists and on the inside of the hocks. Cut the tail skin free from the body skin at the base of the tail. Peel the tail skin back on the tail far enough to give a grip. Set the fingers and thumb-nail of the right hand against the rolled-back tail skin, grip the tail butt with the left hand and strip the tail out of its skin with a strong, even pull both ways.

Straighten the tail skin out, make a small incision on its under-

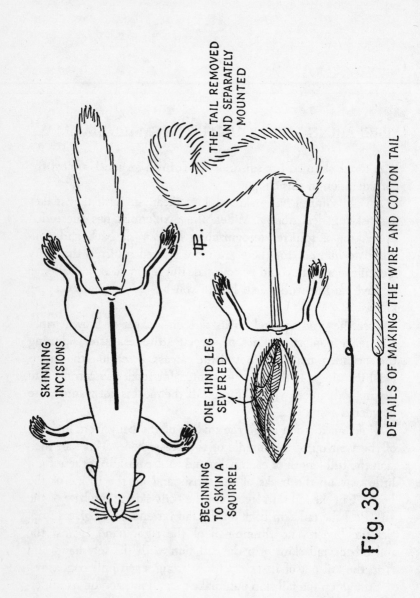

SKINNING
INCISIONS

THE TAIL REMOVED
AND SEPARATELY
MOUNTED

ONE HIND LEG
SEVERED

BEGINNING
TO SKIN A
SQUIRREL

DETAILS OF MAKING THE WIRE AND COTTON TAIL

Fig. 38

side near the tip, and drop the tail skin into borax saturate solution. The tail should be mounted on its wire-and-cotton core separately from the body and dried before assembling on the mount.

Peel the body skin down over the hips. Sever the hip joints and the leg muscles from the pelvis. Hang the squirrel up on the chain-and-hooks, then peel the body skin down over the chest. Sever the fore-legs at the shoulder joints and continue on down over the head. Cut the ear linings deeply in the tubes. Cut the eyelids free close to the skull, as also the lips, so as to keep the linings entire with the skin. Sever the end of the nose close to the skull so as to have the nostril linings complete on the skin.

Split the lips, clean gristle and tissue out of the nose, split the eyelids, and skin the backs of the ears out to their edges. Rub borax into all parts as you go. Skin the legs out down to the toes. Remove meat and tendons from the undersides of the paws and feet. Clean all meat from the leg bones, but do not disarticulate the joints.

Scrape and carefully shear meat and fat from all over the inside of the skin. Rub borax in, then scrape again thoroughly. The skin is now ready for the borax mothproofing bath. Soak it in borax saturate solution for an hour or so, stirring and squeezing it occasionally to facilitate complete saturation. (Red squirrels are to be soaked but briefly, then dusted and fluffed at once, as their pigmentation is soluble.)

Squeeze the skin out of the solution and dust it to complete fluffy condition in dry borax. The specimen may be mounted right away, or it may be dried to keep for another time. If it is to be mounted soon, roll it up in oilcloth while preparations are being made for the work of assembling.

Using the real tail for a model, spin a tapered cotton tail on a wire with its end filed nearly to a point, with a long gradual taper. Rub wax on the tapered portion of the wire before beginning the cotton wrapping. Turn a tight loop in the wire where the butt of the tail will be. Do not make the artificial tail too

75

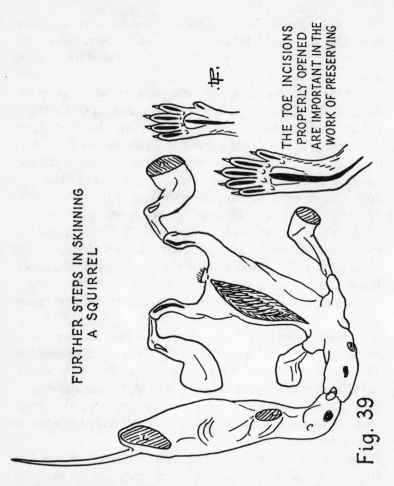

FURTHER STEPS IN SKINNING A SQUIRREL

THE TOE INCISIONS PROPERLY OPENED ARE IMPORTANT IN THE WORK OF PRESERVING

Fig. 39

thick. It should be either exactly the dimensions of the natural tail, or just a shade smaller.

When dusting and fluffing the tail skin, stuff the opening at its butt end with a little wad of paper handkerchief to keep out the powdered borax. When the tail is fluffed, remove the plug, dampen the cotton tail with borax solution, and slip it into place, using care not to twist the skin on it. Sew the butt of the tail skin to the loop in the wire with a few stitches, and tie it snugly.

76

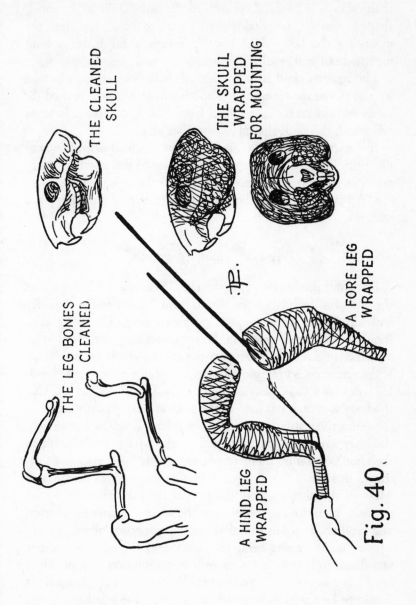

THE CLEANED SKULL

THE SKULL WRAPPED FOR MOUNTING

A FORE LEG WRAPPED

THE LEG BONES CLEANED

A HIND LEG WRAPPED

Fig. 40.

77

If the skin is to be dried for storage, the tail should be mounted, shaped, combed, and dried on its core to await the time for mounting the body skin. By this means a far better-looking mounted tail will result.

The squirrel skull is to be cleaned, boraxed, and kept to take its part in the mounting of the specimen. Whether it is used directly or only serves as a model from which to carve a head of soft wood, the skull should not be discarded.

If the specimen is to be made up into a cabinet skin, the complete skull should accompany it as a part of the essential study material. In such a case, remove the brain through the atlas opening. A brain spoon may be made by hammering and shaping a wire tip.

Preparing mounting assembly

Bring out the brown paper sketches. Measure the legs and cut the wires for them twice the length from the toes to the shoulder and hip joints. These require no sharpening. The body wire should be one size larger than the leg wires. Leg wires need to be of sufficient strength to support the squirrel with no wobbling. If the specimen is to be mounted in an upright position, the hind-leg wires have to be heavier than for the four-footed stance. Cut the body wire twice as long as the neck and body combined.

Secure the natural skull or the artificial head on one end of the body wire. Measure backward on the wire to the position of the shoulder joints, then, one neck length back of this point, turn a small round loop in it, with the loop turned downward. Measure the distance from the base of the neck to the hip-joint position. Here follow the plan in the accompanying illustration and bend a wire pelvis into shape with taper-nosed pliers.

Now is the time to bring the skin out of the oilcloth, or, if it was dried, to sponge it inside with borax solution and stretch it until it is completely relaxed and ready for mounting. Damp skins should be kept refrigerated, but not frozen, if the weather is warm

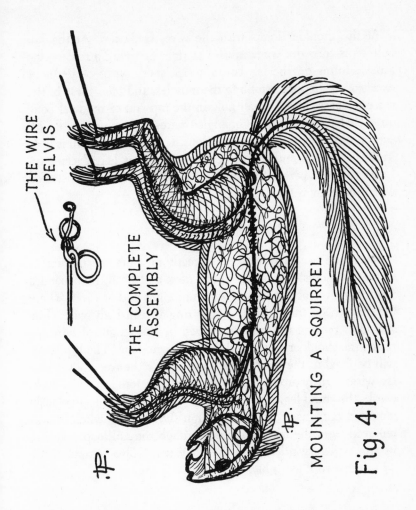

THE WIRE PELVIS

THE COMPLETE ASSEMBLY

MOUNTING A SQUIRREL

Fig. 41

when they are prepared. In any case do not allow them to become heated at all.

Turn the leg skins inside out down to the toes, for attaching the leg wires to the leg bones. Bend the wires to fit along under the leg bones. Bind the wires in place on the bones with thread. Let 3 or 4 inches of wire extend beyond the ends of the paws and feet.

At the shoulder joints turn the wires backward. At the hip ball-joints turn the wires inward at right angles. To replace the muscle forms on the leg bones, pluck small wisps of jewelers' excelsior to shapes resembling the muscles, and bind these in the correct places. Bore a small hole in the top end of the heel bone on each leg and insert right-angled wires lightly wrapped with cotton to replace the Achilles tendons. If the natural skull is used in the head, stuff and wrap on excelsior jaw-muscle replacements. Leave the back part of the thighs unfilled. These are to be stuffed when the body is filled.

Assembling

Insert the head in the skin, correctly measure the placement of the shoulders in relation to the neck and head, then bend a right angle in each fore-limb wire, one right and one left, where they are to go through the single ring in the body wire. The shoulders require the free play given by the length of wire between the shoulder points and the body wire loop. The hip joints will be fixed in the wire pelvis loops. Twist the free ends of the leg wires tightly around the body wire, the fore-leg wires backward, the hind-leg wires forward. Bring out the previously mounted tail. Insert its wire through the opening where it was removed from the body skin and through the tail loop, twisting its free end forward around the body wire. This completes the wire framework assembly.

Stuffing

Moisten the inside of the skin with borax solution. Stuff a few wisps of jewelers' excelsior into the neck, around the base of the skull. Place this first filling with care, to secure a smooth juncture of the head with the neck, then fill the neck skin evenly all around the neck wire.

Lay a long single wad of fine excelsior in the back, between the body wire assembly and the skin. Stuff the backs of the thighs to their natural shape with fine excelsior.

Stuff the chest and abdomen to their full proportions. Press and mold the filling to natural shape. Sew up the body incision, from the rear toward the front end, using short stitches and drawing up each two or three tightly as you move along. Before entirely completing the sewing, check the stuffing to make sure no more is required.

Fill the paws and feet with a little papier-mâché to replace the flesh of palms and soles. As each is filled, sew up the incision, beginning at its outer end.

Drill holes to receive the leg wires in the perch or base. Shape the squirrel somewhat into the attitude chosen, and mount it on the perch.

Mounting and finishing

Draw the leg wires down snugly under the perch, and clinch them to hold the feet in contact. Complete shaping the specimen. Feel it all over, from tail to head, and press out all lumpiness. Set a darning needle in a needle-vise and use this to prod through the skin and pry the filling up under the left palm to completely re-arrange all hollow or lumpy spots in the body.

Pin the toes to grasp the perch naturally. Keep the head wrapped in cloth dampened with borax solution until the rest of the specimen is finished.

If the squirrel is to be sitting up holding a nut, drill opposite holes in the nut-shell. Cut off the paw wires just long enough to go barely through the nut, turn the paws to holding position with the wires bent at right angles to them, then first press the paws directly together with the wires passing and spring them apart enough to insert the wires through the nut. Clinch the short wire ends down on opposite sides of the nut. Shape the paws around the nut naturally, and bind them on the nut with a few turns of cotton cops.

Uncover the head. Make a small incision in the ears inside of their front flanges, where the cut will not show. Put a little papier-mâché through the incisions to fill the ears and enough to fill the ear butts; mold the ears to their natural shape. Fill the eye sockets with papier-mâché and set the glass eyes without bulginess. Use a needle point to shape the eyelids around the eyes. Pin the corners of the eyes with small needles or insect pins. Fill the nose and lips with just enough papier-mâché to bring them up to natural form. Live squirrels do not show more than the tips of the long front teeth, and their upper lips are flat and extended. A few insect pins will be of help in holding the lip and nose details in place until dried. Papier-mâché should be mixed rather thick for finishing the face and foot details. Comb the tail and body hair.

When the squirrel is completely dried out, wax the eyelids and inside of the lips. Comb the fur and touch up the perch with a little color.

CHAPTER VII

PREPARING AND MOUNTING A TORTOISE, A HORNED TOAD, AND A CRAYFISH

A tortoise

While this writer does not favor the indiscriminate slaughter of turtles and tortoises for taxidermy use, occasionally a fine specimen does turn up as a temptation. When one thinks of the great array of them that lie in the "pickle" jars of museums, he can hardly be condemned for taking an occasional specimen. Pond turtles, at any rate, are frowned upon by our best conservation authorities.

The following method of tortoise preparation does away with cutting the shell apart. Make all of the incisions along the underside of the neck, legs, and tail. Cut the lower edge of the body skin free from the plastron, leaving enough edge to sew to, from the neck incision outward to each fore-leg incision—not beyond. Do the same from the tail incision outward to each hind-leg incision. Skin the neck and base of the head, and the legs and tail, leaving the leg bones and the skull attached to the skin. Clean all meat from the leg bones and skull, removing the eyeballs, jaw meat, and brain. Do not disarticulate the joints, except at the shoulder and hip attachments in the shell. Clean out the contents of the shell. A long-handled scraper is handy for this work. Be sure to get the dorsal meat out of the roof of the shell. Rub the specimen inside and out with powdered borax, and spread it out on its back to dry completely before attempting the mounting. When once it is well dried, do not moisten the shell again.

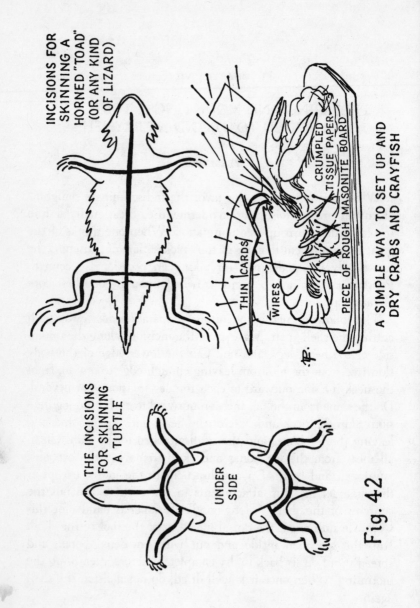

INCISIONS FOR SKINNING A HORNED "TOAD" (OR ANY KIND OF LIZARD)

THE INCISIONS FOR SKINNING A TURTLE

UNDER SIDE

THIN CARDS

WIRES

CRUMPLED TISSUE PAPER

PIECE OF ROUGH MASONITE BOARD

A SIMPLE WAY TO SET UP AND DRY CRABS AND CRAYFISH

Fig. 42

When ready to begin mounting, melt a sizable pot of wax. Dip wads of fine excelsior into the hot wax, then drain and lay them on damp paper to cool. When ready for mounting, relax the skin by applying borax solution to it repeatedly until it is pliable. Make neck and tail cores by spinning cotton on wires cut long enough for anchorage through the shell stuffing. Apply the leg wires to the bones in the same way as in mounting a squirrel. Sharpen the inner ends of all six wires. Wrap plucked excelsior muscle cores on the legs, binding them smoothly with thread.

Stuff the shell full of the waxed excelsior, leaving a hollow at front and back ends to receive the legs, neck, and tail. Push the neck and fore-leg wires backward through the body stuffing and clinch the wire ends back into the stuffing at the rear end. Push the hind-leg and tail wires forward through the body stuffing, and clinch the ends into the stuffing at the front end.

Cover the neck, leg, and tail cores with papier-mâché. Sew up all incisions with short stitches. Sew the lower edge of the body skin to the corresponding edge of skin left along the front and rear of the plastron, where it was cut free. Perforate the skin of the neck, legs, and tail all over between the scales with a three-cornered needle to allow the papier-mâché to dry out. Mount the tortoise on its base. Fill the eye sockets with papier-mâché, and set the glass eyes. Slit the nose skin a little, scrape and clean out the cartilage, and stuff the nose with cotton, adjusting the nostrils to dry into natural form. When dried, any shrinkage should be replaced with wax.

Mold the neck, legs, and tail details, and set the specimen aside to dry. Look it over occasionally, and mold the details while drying to insure against warping.

When dry, replace the faded colors with oil paints, linseed oil, and turpentine.

A horned toad

Make a full-length ventral, tail, body, and neck incision. Make full-length incisions on underside of the legs. Skin the specimen carefully, leaving the leg bones attached at the feet and the skull in place, with the jaw meat and eyes cleaned out. Make a contact outline of the skinned body to use as a pattern for the artificial body. Shape the flat body from fine excelsior. Wire, then wrap the leg bones and tail with a little excelsior. Assemble the specimen in the same manner as a bird is put together. Cover the body, leg, and tail cores with papier-mâché. Sew up the body incision first, beginning at the end of the tail, then sew up the legs. Perforate the skin all over between the scales with a three-cornered needle. Set the lizard on its base, and mold the skin and papier-mâché together. Pin the toes into natural position. Set aside to dry thoroughly. Replace skin colors same as for the tortoise mount. When coloring a specimen, use as little paint as possible, to get the natural appearance.

A crayfish

Crayfish, crabs, etc., may be killed in borax saturate solution for mounting. When they are dead, perforate all of the joint membranes with a three-cornered needle, then soak again in the borax solution for an hour or so. Drain thoroughly.

Pose the mounts in natural attitudes held up by the aid of excelsior or crumpled tissue paper and pins or sharpened wires, and dry them completely. Color them as recommended for the previous specimens.

Starfishes

Take live starfishes from the sea-water and lay them on a board until collapsed; then immerse them while alive in formalin solution until they swell to natural shape and harden. (Dead starfishes cannot inhale and assume their natural forms when immersed in the formalin.)

Remove the starfishes from the formalin and drain them well, so that the solution returns to its container. Dry them on a board, turning them over occasionally so that the drying will be uniform. Dried starfishes may be bugproofed by being briefly immersed in borax solution, then re-dried.

Replace natural colors of the dried starfishes with oil paints, applied thinly. When handling formalin specimens, keep the hands from contact with the solution.

CHAPTER VIII

PAPIER-MÂCHÉS, PASTES, MOTHPROOFING SOLUTION, ETC.

Several ready-to-mix, commercial, dry papier-mâché compounds are offered by the trade. Many are made from tried and proven formulas, and they save a great deal of work and worry for the taxidermist.

Skin pastes of standard composition are also sold, to the advantage of the user. Casein glue may be made up and extended with flour paste for a practical skin paste.

Paper pulp, finely chopped tow, or cotton sheared to ¼ or ⅛ inch long may be added to the casein glue and flour paste mixture to make it into papier-mâché. White or cream-colored casein water paint may be moistened with water to a rather thick paste, left for fifteen minutes, then mixed with chopped tow, to make a practical papier-mâché. Make only an amount that will be used up the same day. The long-winded papier-mâché formulas of bygone times are largely obsolete, along with arsenical mothproofing and hay stuffing.

Borax-solution immersion followed by dry borax dusting and fluffing of skins brings to the art of taxidermy its greatest boon—mothproofing that will not kill the operator.

To make borax saturate solution, four ounces of powdered borax per gallon of cool water is required. Stir the water briskly while sifting in the borax. Six ounces to the gallon may be recommended so that the operator visualizes the fact of full-strength absorption of the chemical by seeing a deposit of unassimilated powder on the bottom of the container.

88

Do not leave skins lying endlessly in borax solution. Borax solution may be re-used until it becomes dirty, but fairly clean solution is desirable for retaining the fresh look of specimens. Borax purchased in hundred-pound lots from the producer costs under four dollars, so that no worry about its expensiveness need be entertained.

Borax is an ideal feather and fur-dusting powder, and can be used over and over indefinitely. It does not bleach colors. Any liquid will dissolve and re-assemble color pigmentation in some kinds of skins, such as the red squirrel.

THE END.

INDEX